T0064418

Explore
the Philosophy of Achievers
within You

Make
Your
Dreams
Come True

By the Chosen One: Mahesh Chandnani

PARTRIDGE
A Penguin Random House Company

ISBN: Hardcover   978-1-4828-5897-6
            Softcover   978-1-4828-5896-9
            eBook   978-1-4828-5895-2

Print information available on the last page.

To order additional copies of this book, contact
Partridge India
000 800 10062 62
orders.india@partridgepublishing.com

www.partridgepublishing.com/india

MESSAGE TO YOU

Message to You

Every individual living in this world has taken birth in this world with a purpose that is attached to their life. The purpose of life is determined by the surrounding, in which we are born. The family in which we first open our eyes to is given to us by our destiny. Our destiny is something which we all bring along with us. It comes to us when we take our first breath inside our mother's womb. We all humans have a pre-defined destiny. The fact is that our Destiny is ready for us even before we are born to this beautiful world. Fetus inside the womb takes a 9 month process to be born sometimes we also have premature births happening around 7th month of pregnancy. It is all determined by the Destiny, what it has written for us, it happens accordingly. Have you ever imagined, how the baby is going to be like, how the baby is going to look like, what character the baby is going to have, how the baby is going to progress in life etc. Everything about the baby's life is already mentioned in his destiny.

You may feel, what I m telling you about baby's appearance is determined by the parents Deoxyribonucleic acid, commonly known as DNA. DNA determines the characteristics of the baby, it also emphasizes on baby's appearance. But the main important thing DNA classifies for the baby is the sex, whether the baby is going to be a girl or a boy. It completely depends on the father's genetics which gets interchanged with mother's genetics forming a new genetic structure which has the combination of both parent genetics.

For example

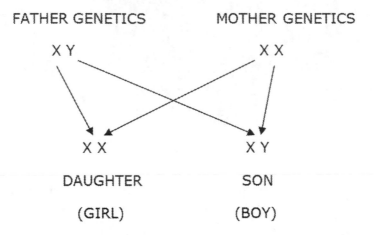

FATHER GENETICS   MOTHER GENETICS

X Y   X X

X X   X Y

DAUGHTER   SON

(GIRL)   (BOY)

This is how DNA helps us determining sex of the unborn or in other words this is how science explains us how sex is determined for the baby during the time of conception. There is something beyond science that makes this process happen naturally and it is baby's Destiny. Destiny of the baby knows the sex of the baby even before the conception takes place. If the baby's Destiny has a role of being a Man then the conception will take place with XY genetics eventually leading to a baby boy and if the Destiny has a role of being a Woman then the conception of XX genetics will take place leading to a baby girl. Science may say that it is DNA that determines sex for the baby but actually it is our destiny which has chosen a life for us and is responsible for making us be a girl or a boy.

Destiny for us has everything we have had since birth, followed by the life we are living to whatever we are going to have in our future. Our Destiny has everything planned for us right from the first breathe till we take our last. From our birth day to our last day of life everything is known by the destiny. We do not get to choose when our birthday should be nor do we get to choose when we will die, it all is a part of Destiny and we cannot change it, but what we humans try to change in our destiny is the phase between our birth and death which is known as LIFE.

We humans try to control something which is already written for us in our destiny. Instead of accepting our life the way it is we want to mold it according to our own convenience, making it a lot more difficult to live. We reject what is good for us and try to manipulate life comparing it with others. This makes us go far from being who we are because we try to become like others around us. Every person in this world has been given enough of everything that would be required for living a peaceful life. But we humans always want what we do not have in our life. It is we who have to let things be as they are to achieve all we want in our life. Tricky isn't it but the truth is, if we try to manipulate our destiny by overpowering it, it will lead us to a phase of life where we aren't happy. As the happiness for us has become a temporary emotion which is gained by achieving things that we did not have, this kind of situation happens to all and it is very addictive in nature. Whole life we spend searching happiness in things that we want in our life and the list never ends. Every day we develop a new interest towards a particular thing and believe that once I have achieved that I will become happy, but sadly it does not happen. It is our fault as we think we rule the world, while choosing what is best for us, ignoring the fact that there is something present high above us, who has given us a life with a destiny that is specially written for it. Destiny act as a guide for us from the time we are born till the time we die. What makes us away from our own destiny which GOD has planned for us is our own **EGO**.

Everybody in this world suffer with this human problem called EGO. It is EGO which makes us feel unhappy all the time. It is the reason why we make our own life miserable and suffer from unwanted sadness. If you wonder how everything is disturbed and affected in our life because of three letter word EGO. Then you would be interested in knowing how it all happens, why our happiness is converted into frustrations and what makes EGO take us away from our destiny.

**I will explain you everything you want to know
about life in the following sequence**

"It takes efforts to finish your work but it requires an extra effort to make your work a success"

– Mahesh Chandnani

Contents

Acknowledgement

I as an Author am thankful to god who has chosen me to spread awareness among his people, helping them understand the long lost philosophy of human mankind. I am thankful to my holy guardian angel who has guided me to write this book properly.

I am thankful to my Destiny for making me capable of leading an inspiration to thousands of people, with whom I share this hidden philosophy. It wouldn't have been possible for me to know all the things I have written in this book if it wouldn't have been in my Destiny.

I thank all my mentors who have helped me first discover true potential in me, as it was their teachings which first brought me closer to myself and helped me understand life.

I would like to thank all the heavenly relatives who have bestowed their blessings over me, specially my GRANDFATHER who was very dear to me.

I would like to thank my Fiancée DIVYA BACHWANI who has been the back bone for me. I had first shared this knowledge with her and with her support I have been able to climb all the steps leading to complete this book. Her strong believe in me has made me publish this book that is going to change lives for millions of readers worldwide.

I would like to thank my parents PRAKASH CHANDNANI AND ANITA CHANDNANI for educating me as I can't imagine myself being able to write this book without any education. Their support for me has been there always and they have always helped me during my struggles of life.

I would like to thank all other people who have directly or indirectly helped in my journey of life where I have experienced all the mentioned things and have shared all that I have learnt from it.

I would like to thank all the living beings who have contributed in making my book reach to you as it is their efforts that has only made all this possible. All the people have worked together as a team and has made me achieve this dream.

Lastly I would like to thank you as a reader, for believing in this book. As it is your fate which has made you to buy this book knowing the fact that reading this book is going to change your life.

"You are the master in exploring your own destiny"

- Mahesh Chandnani

Introduction

I was fifteen when I was first introduced to the process of changing our Reality. It was in 2007 when I had finished my school and was about to enter high school, my parents had put me for a personality development program as according to them I was shy in nature and I had a fear of talking in front of people so to overcome that I was doing this short term course on public speaking as well.

I yet remember it was my last day of that program when my sir (An 83 year old retired army officer) came to me and said

"If you have to change your life, you will have to read books and apply what your learn from them"

He wrote three books for me, first on SUBCONCIOUS MIND, second on LAW OF ATTRACTION and third on HOW TO WIN IN LIFE.

I had never read any books apart from academics but now I had 3 books in hand that would eventually decide my future. Regardless of knowing how it would help me, I decided to start reading my first book on subconscious mind. Days passed by, months passed by, but I struggled daily to understand the whole concept behind the process of subconscious mind. Soon came a day when I finished reading the book but the mind was full of doubts as I yet couldn't understand how everything works. It took me 6 months to finish this book but the concepts were not clear. With a lost mind I stared reading the second book from the list which was on attraction. This was a miracle that I was able to understand both the books with reference of one and other. Since then I have been using techniques learnt from both the books together and it made more sense to actually understand how it was working together rather trying to understand them separately. Making me over confident about knowing life, I started ignoring the books thinking I knew what was in them. This attitude of mine stopped me from reading the third book which was about winning in life. As a boy who wanted to know what life is, I had started thinking that I knew life like nobody else. My overconfidence made me suffer in life as it was my EGO that made me feel superior than others and also boosted me about knowing everything I wanted to know about life, by just reading first book and half of the second I started to believe that I knew life.

Life moved on, I struggled with education. I was dropped out from my high school at the age of 17. There was a lot of shame involved as nobody had ever failed in my family before and it was a new thing in my family. To cover up this shame I started working, one year I was working as a fitness Instructor at a gym but this didn't work either. I had to leave that job and later was jobless for nearly 3 months thinking what to do next in life.

I thought the best way to work is to have your own business, at the age of 18 I had my own catering firm, it became a family business later, where I and my mom both used to handle this business. We earned great revenues from it but after a year the orders started reducing, making us experience a downfall of the market, struggling to achieve profits we eventually had to end it. Life had shown me enough of struggle already I was just 19 by this time. A normal 19 year old boy is just enjoying his college life but I was lost somewhere in life where I didn't know what to do. I was experiencing a harsh phase of life which was leading me to go into depression. I might have lost all hopes in life if my parents had not put me back to high school so that I could complete my education. It was year 2010 when I was back in high school, frankly after the harsh life full of failures the new start in high school as a student was so relaxed all I had to do was attend lectures, enjoy with friends, study and pass in exams, etc. Interestingly, I liked my life as a student compared to my previous hardships. I had few more struggles in my education later, but now thankfully I am a graduate and have pursued my career as a full time Author and I m focused on making this Author industry a better place for student writers all over the world. I believe that students all over the world should be given a better platform to showcase their work among people. This is my ultimate dream to be achieved in life.

"Dreams can be achieved by focusing on the map required to reach our destination"

- Mahesh Chandnani

The hidden philosophy

You may be wondering why I m sharing with you my life experiences as a part of introduction for this book. I would explain how all this, is a part of introduction to you, with the help of examples.

We create all what happens in our life. May it be good or may it be bad, whatever it is that you are going through right now is because of you. You are the creator of your own happiness and sorrows. We all do this knowingly or unknowingly in our life.

When something goes wrong in our life suddenly we always hear our self complaining about things which we didn't wanted. Other commonly seen phenomenon is when you ask God WHY ME? The brain always ask this question as it is curious to know why only me is getting affected with problems and bad fortune while we see others enjoying in life. This is what brain thinks while our heart always notifies us about something bad which is going to happen or gives us a signal about things which are wrong. These both situations happens to us simultaneously as the first it is the brain that is confused about the whole situation while second is our heart that calms us down showing us the path which helps us to choose the right thing in life.

Our heart always knows what is good for us and what is bad. It is the brain that always overpowers the notion of our heart. We end up taking a wrong decision which leads us to a wrong turn in life. Making our journey of life difficult, we end up being sad and frustrated, wanting the change that will lead us to happiness. We survive waiting to find happiness until the hope for living dies within.

Imagine if you're travelling in a car and you have to travel from location A to destination B. if you plan your journey properly you would know the path that would lead you there properly. But if we take a wrong turn while driving and continue going you would end up on a different route, you will have to change your routes again to come on the right path that would lead you to the correct destination. This same thing happens in life when we take a wrong turn which makes us go far from our destination. This leads us to live a life which is not satisfactory. We feel stuck in a situation that we no longer can change the only thing we have in our hands is to go back from where we had started and plan out things again from scratch so that with the second chance we can choose the right path. Not many people can do this as they find it risky to start their life again as they have Responsibilities and liabilities attached with them.

You may understand this looking at this picture.

The figure will explain you how we plan to reach from location A to destination B choosing path 1. If we take a wrong turn choosing path 3 and 4 we can never reach our destination B but if we take a wrong turn choosing path 2 then we can alter our paths eventually leading us towards destination B. Similar things happen in our life as well. When we overpower our inner saying we choose the wrong path. We all know what is inside us. We all have our inner conscious that whispers things to us. Our brain overpowers our inner conscious by saying 'we know what is right for us' even though our heart says it's wrong we choose the wrong thing for us. We trap ourselves leading our own way without knowing where to go. It is very important to know the destination as it helps us take the right path in life. Generally people take life as it comes to them, this way of living is an lazy attitude towards life as today you wish to live, tomorrow you will survive but day after you may not feel worth living again the same yesterday. Such people end up wasting their lives as they aimlessly keep on moving to various places taking one turn after the other, sometimes they even reach the same place from where they had started their journey. All I am trying to explain here is that we all need to have a life which has a destination to reach or else we tend to lose ourselves while making the journey.

We face problems in life because of our careless attitude towards it. We take life as it comes but never take responsibility to take things in control.

If I tell you today that tomorrow we are going for a trip. We have our tickets ready and the flight is tomorrow morning at 4:30am. I will pick you up from your house at 1am, we will reach airport in half an hour. We will then collect are tickets and boarding pass, lastly we would check in our flight.

Whatever information I have given you above is accurate information. It makes you ready for the process and now you know what you have to do so that you are ready when I would come to pick you.

Unfortunately nobody tells us what we have to do in our life. There is no accurate information to be followed. All we know is that we are breathing and we will live our life till our last breath. We are not guided in life by anyone. Everyone just shares their life experiences with us and we learn from them or sometimes we create a new experience altogether, but there is something inside us that always tries its level best to guide us, you may call it your inner voice, your subconscious mind, your soul, your guardian angel, your hearts notion, your spirituality etc. You may call it anything but for everyone in this world there is something within you that knows you much better than you know yourself in life.

It is really important to know our journey as we are the guide of our own life. We all have one life to live and we all have to do so many things in life. But did you know all these years we have lived a lie. Whatever we know in life is the world outside us but we have never explored the world within us.

"We all human beings have the power to achieve everything we want in our life it is in our destiny to become successful in life"

– Mahesh Chandnani

Yes it is true you can be successful in your life and achieve everything you want to achieve in life by following the simple steps you will learn reading this book. When you learn to apply these things to your life you will explore the magic that has always been present within you.

But the question I want to ask you now is

ARE YOU WILLING TO CHANGE YOUR LIFE?
DO YOU REALLY WANT TO BE SUCCESSFUL?
WILL YOU FOLLOW THINGS THAT WILL GRANT YOU ALL YOUR WISHES?
ARE YOU READY FOR NEW WAY OF LIVING?

If all your answers are yes then I will make you explore the hidden philosophy behind achieving success, power, money, name, fame, love, health, happiness, prosperity, abundance, peace etc

Almost everything can be earned and achieved with this philosophy

Let's get to know the hidden philosophy that is there behind achieving all you want in your life in the next chapter.

PHILOSOPHY OF ACHIEVERS

"If you can Dream it
You can ACHIEVE it
All the POWER lies
WITHIN YOU"

- Mahesh Chandnani

Philosophy Of Achievers

Philosophy of achiever is where you can learn how to achieve everything you want in your life by applying few simple steps that helps you understand the power that is present within you.

This philosophy has been present in the world since the beginning of human mankind. Very few people in this world are able to achieve this hidden philosophy that has made them discover their destination and has also helped them in making their path towards it. All the other people are unaware of this philosophy because it cannot be shared. We can only achieve it practicing ourselves. We all know the philosophy it is with us since we are born. The true fact is that we do not have to go anywhere to get this philosophy as it is WITHIN us.

To understand this philosophy you need to know yourself apart from your name, family, address, friends, likes, dislikes, attachments, memories, emotions, body, etc. **Do you know who you are?**

You have spend so many years of your life but **Do you know for what purpose you were born?**

Purpose of life does not mean what job you do or how much money you make. Purpose of your life is directly related to your destiny. Very few chosen once become aware of their main purpose of living while others struggle their entire life hoping for their destiny to change miraculously. People who do not try to understand their purpose of life are left aloof by this world as they can't understand what they are living for but they are living to find something.

This something is nothing else but the destination which is hidden from them because they are searching for it in a wrong direction of life.

These people are those whom we see every day in the morning, running behind busses trains or cabs wanting to reach their work place. These people are so busy with their daily activities that they no longer have time to listen to what their heart wants to tell them. Time is money for these people and making money becomes their ultimate goal in life. These people spend their entire life making money and when they retire they spend all the money or sometimes they end up even spending more then what they have earned in their lifespan.

Life isn't about making money or the struggle that follows behind making money. Life has many more beautiful things attached to it other than money. Money is just one aspect of life which is given the most importance. No doubt money is necessary but it isn't the ultimate goal for living. You may wonder how will you survive without money but the truth is money is not used for survival. To survive we only need 3 necessary things in life that is food clothing and shelter. Money isn't mentioned in these 3 necessities of life. Money is manmade it was not existing before. All man made things make humans dependent on them and we crave for more.

This is how money is classified in our society

A poor man works for survival as he wants to eat food from the money he earns every day.

A middle class man earns money to save up for his living, so that if he is spending half of his income on buying new things he likes or spends on travelling he has the other half of his income kept for him to rely on during the time of emergencies.

A rich man treats money like he treats any other thing in his life. For instance, if the rich man is hungry he eats food and if he wants money he makes more money without any struggles involved.

What we do in our life is that we have emotions, fear, sacrifice, sentiments, feelings etc attached with money. This leads us to a panic situation. We ask ourselves if I don't earn, what will happen to my life? If I m not working for money who will pay my debts? How can I survive without money?

The answer is nobody cares about how you live, what you work, etc. everybody around you is just worried about how much money you make for living. The quantity of income is determined as the quality of an individual. Other aspects of life are simply ignored because money is given importance.

It's a kind of pressure that builds up in our society where you have to follow what everyone else is doing. That is 'working for living' people take up jobs spend each day of their life working for that same job until they realize that their life has passed by and all they have left with themselves is their old age and their medications to survive. If you have a job and are happy with your job then it's a different story as your job has become your destination and there is nothing beyond it for you. You are not at all interested in exploring other things in life as you want to spend your entire day, weeks, months, and years going to your office. You consider yourself satisfied with what you get from your life. Being satisfied with life is the first step that stops you from growing in life.

"Life is an adventure live it like a RIDE"

– Mahesh Chandnani

I am not indicating you to leave your job or trap yourself into another mess. All I m trying to say is one should have a purpose in life, a destination that can lead you to live a meaningful life.

Having a purpose to live adds meaning to your life

If the purpose is missing our life becomes meaningless. We are just spending days after days without knowing what our purpose in our life is.

If you go watch a movie and you like it for the first time. You will enjoy the same movie watching it the second time. You may feel ok watching it the third time, but would definitely get bored watching it the fourth time. If I ask you to see the same movie again for the fifth time, you wouldn't be interested. This happens to us because we like to explore new things in life. We get fascinated doing the same thing as an adventure, second time. Doing the same thing again gives us joy, the third time experience is great because we have already done it twice before. But later if you do the same thing again for the fourth time it is going to be an automated process as we learnt the new thing first time felt amazed doing it the second time and mastered it doing it again for the third time. This new thing is no longer new for us as it has gone down to our subconscious mind. We can now do the same thing again and again without paying much of attention because of subconscious mind.

This is how life is, everything we learn new becomes dull after doing it fourth time in life as what you learnt for the first time has been mastered by you doing it repeatedly for three to four times. The adventure has been explored and it is no longer new for us to do it again. That is why it gets shifted to subconscious mind. Let me explain you the philosophy behind the **subconscious mind.**

Subconscious mind in our body plays a very important role helping us live our daily life. The things we do daily or have an experience doing it more than five times in our life is now controlled by the subconscious mind. How much ever time the same thing is repeated in our life it is the subconscious mind that help us do the same thing 10,100,200,500,1000,5000 or 10000 times in life.

Every day we get up take the brush in the hand and start brushing our teeth's without being aware of the fact that we have not been awake properly. We brush our teeth's while our conscious mind is still sleeping. How does this happen, how is it that we always spend our life doing so many things without being aware of them. It happens with the help of subconscious mind. When we are walking on the road wondering about our thoughts we automatically reach a place where we had to go. This is also because of the subconscious mind. When we drive a car listening to songs, our conscious mind is busy singing the same song over and over again while the driving controls are taken over by the subconscious mind, assuring our safety while we rejoice our memories with favorite song.

It is like the auto pilot system which is used in the planes where the pilot after reaching the desired altitude keeps the plain on auto pilot and sits back monitoring it. Same thing is seen in our life when our conscious mind gets busy with the thoughts our general activities are controlled by our auto pilot (subconscious mind). Let me give you an example

The sudden brakes which we apply when someone comes in front of our car, it is subconscious mind.

Things once grasped by our subconscious mind are there with us for life time. Think about it you learned to cycle when you were young and now suddenly after having no practice of ridding cycle for so many years, if I give you a cycle to ride you will be able to ride it exactly how you used to ride without any problems as it would be the subconscious mind that will take control over it.

Same goes for driving, swimming, etc. all these things are learnt once in life but it stays with us forever without any problems we can swim or drive or ride like we used to, when we had first learnt it. It is like a song we download and store on our computer hard drive we can store it until we wish to delete it from our hard drive, but deleting a memory from a subconscious mind is undoable.

We can forget the memory but it is always stored inside us, if stressed a lot we can recollect many memories which we had almost forgotten. The new memories which are created every now and then are piled upon the old memories making these old memories go down and down the memory lane. How much ever the memory goes down it is still going to be a memory that can always be any time remembered by the subconscious mind in our life.

This is how subconscious mind is important for human beings as it does 80% of the daily work for them. Carrying all the memories whether good or bad with it, the subconscious mind always takes care of human beings. It helps them identify the different situations of life by comparing them to the memory that's attached with previous experiences.

Subconscious mind keeps a track of every emotion that is attached with different situations of life. For example we have happy memories, sad memories, good memories, bad memories, etc. All these memories that are stored inside us have these following emotions attached with it.

Fear	Anticipation
Anger	Calmness
Sadness	Happiness
Envy	Confidence
Enmity	Trust
Cruelty	Kindness
Expectation	Surprise
Hate	Love

**Each memory has one or more emotion attached with
it and it is stored in our subconscious mind.**

Your first day at work, your first friend in college, last time you were sad, your first crush, your last flirt, your last day in school, etc these are your memories which all have an emotion attached. These first and last moments of our life have more impact in our life compared to our daily memories. You may think that it is our conscious mind which takes care of memory for us but it isn't the case as our conscious mind is only active when we are awake but our subconscious mind is 24 hrs, 365days always active. That is why we are able to remember dreams which we see during our sleep as they are again stored in our subconscious mind.

Right from the day we are born till the day we die all the memories are stored within us. It is also believed that these memories travel along with us to our next birth, forming our life linked with them.

The first book read by me at the age of 15 was the book on subconscious mind. This book thought people, how they can deliberately use the power of subconscious mind to cater all human wants. When subconscious mind was first revealed to me I was dazzled by the stuffs we could do using our powerful subconscious mind. It seemed like a miracle when, whatever we said to our subconscious mind, would appear in front of us.

For example: if you want to meet somebody you would actually repeat in your mind 'I should accidently meet that person today' nearly 100 times in a day until your wish come true.

This technique of subconscious mind is mainly used by parents to teach their children manners and by doctors all over the world when we are sick. As they tell you 'you will be alright soon' this constant repetition helps in calming your conscious mind which is under panic situation because of your illness. This makes your recovery a faster process.

The technique of subconscious mind is actually a deliberate attempt made by the conscious mind making it a daily routine so that the memory gets sink into the subconscious mind and stays forever. Exactly same way our subconscious mind is used by us to gain all the things which we do not have.

Let me give you another example to make it clear.

You are walking on the road and you see someone driving a brand new car in front of you. The constant stare at the car makes you feel happy about the whole moment and the desire of having one such car in your life comes in your mind. This idea of having this brand new car in your life along with the emotion 'happiness' becomes a memory, which then gets stored in our subconscious mind. This is just a memory which is stored under happiness section of our subconscious mind. When you return home later that day sitting on your bed you just recollect this very memory and feel happy about the whole situation. In order to make it happen using subconscious mind you will have to recollect the same memory at least two to three times a day and along with the recollecting process you will have to recite 'I am capable enough to buy this car in my life' as many times as possible. This will help you believe that someday you will be capable enough to own this vehicle in your life.

This process of subconscious mind has only 50:50 chances of making your dream come true as it is mainly used to make you feel confident about your dreams and make you able to achieve them. But the subconscious mind is not

100% accurate and it also goes wrong in understanding what you truly want in life resulting in improper manifestations.

Remember in the introduction, I have mentioned that I was dropped out of high school and had started working at a gym, and later used the money I had earned to start my own business. It was a part of my destiny that all these years I struggled to understand why it all happened but when I came to know what it was, I realized that it was created by me using the subconscious mind. The technique of subconscious mind was used by me unknowing the fact that it would result in an improper manifestation going against me.

I was born and raised in a middle class family, where the entire family is dependent on one person's income. I have seen my dad work all his life doing service for others. Though he has a good post in a nice company now but it wasn't the same case before. It was his experience of all kind of struggles that gave him this deserving post. Higher the post longer the time one has to spend in office.

As a kid I always told myself that when I grow up I do not want to be like my dad. As he hardly gets time to spend with his family as he is busy doing work and work all day long and even on holidays. That was the reason why my life had to see so much of struggles so early in my teens. I yet remember that time when I had to choose from education or work, I had chosen to work because for me even education would also result in working. Becoming a graduate for me then was to become able to seek jobs. With my father's example I always used to pray I will do something other than becoming educated and working for someone else. This is why I had lost interest in education as I believed educating myself would lead me to be like my dad. If education leads to work then why to waste 3 to 4 more years of life on education, when you can work and earn in that same period of time.

Dropping out of high school was an achievement for me. It was a kind of self leading way to success, where I was happy to see myself being categorized with the famous successful people who have become millionaires after being dropped out from their high school or college. I used to look up to these worldwide famous examples of people who were not good at academics but have made history and have written their names with golden letters. Few of these people whom I desired to be then were Steve jobs, bill gates, Dhirubhai Ambani, Mark Zuckerburg etc. I wanted to be as successful as these people were and this was what I used to recite 100 times daily. The thought of becoming successful like these people used to always be in my mind and was consciously repeated by me throughout the day. When my results were out and my name wasn't on the list of passing I felt proud because I believed I had brought myself one step closer in becoming as famous as above mentioned people. I was unaware then that all this was being created by me subconsciously. I used to wake up every morning and look the posters of these people asking 'to be like them'. I wanted to make my name having my own business when I didn't know anything at all about business. I wanted to be famous as these people without doing anything. I had forgotten that it was their passion and their hard work which made all these people famous worldwide. Without being aware of such things I had created something unwanted for me which made my life miserable for that period of time.

Unknowingly I created something which wasn't required and messed up my life by manifesting things wrongly. My mistake then was a blessing now as It helped me discover how the power of subconscious mind can be used against ourselves.

Subconscious mind is very essential for living as it teaches us how to be strong and confident when we talk about achieving our dreams. It can be used by everyone to get what they want but the process isn't 100 % accurate. Subconscious mind is best used to recollect thousands of memories created by us every now and then as they are stored within it.

You may notice that not all our desires get fulfilled. All the things you want are not given to you but all the things you need are always made available.

Let me give you an example to make it clear to you. When we go to a temple church or a mosque without being aware of god's existence we pray to him asking forgiveness for our sins. We also put up a list of things we want in our life in front of him, many a times we do this process subconsciously unknowing the results of it. We blindly follow the process known as Praying.

Prayers are thought to us by our parents and teachers, they are offered to god every day. Even you in your childhood have recited prayers. Every child in school has thought how to pray to GOD. Prayers have existed right from the ancient times. Every soul that existed in this world once knows how to pray. A prayer is nothing else but the process of reciting what we want in our life to god.

Irrespective of your religion we all humans do this, we all choose what we want in our life and rejects what is unwanted even an Atheist does this in life.

A prayer is a conscious effort of asking things from god, which is repeated again and again. Every single line of the prayer gets sink with your subconscious mind and the power of subconscious mind manifests what you had prayed for. This makes you believe that your prayers are answered by almighty and you start praying for more things.

"Life plays different music everyday and we have to dance on its Rhythm, so let us just wear our dancing shoes and be ready, as the next time life comes with a different song, we dance like super stars showing the world WHO WE ARE"

- Mahesh Chandnani

Think about you as a child. What you did to make yourself happy?, who were your friends?, where did you live?, how did you spent all your time?, who spoke to you most in your family?, what did you love to eat then?, how were your school days? What was your favorite subject in school?, which teacher was the best?, what sports had you played?, who was your favorite sports man?, what were your hobbies?, whom you admired that time? Which of these memories mentioned above are most valuable?, if I ask you to pick one memory which you think is on the top of all other memories, you wouldn't be able to choose one best memory. Go ahead read them all again and choose the best one you can. I am sure you would be confused what to choose and what not to choose. This is happening to you because all these questions are from your golden period of life called **CHILDHOOD.** We all experience childhood in a different manner but these questions remain the same for all. You can add as many questions you want to the list. They would be common for all the only thing that would change would be the answers as we all humans have had a different childhood. Your answers would be different then mine as we both have different childhood experiences. Childhood experiences come from the background in which we were brought up. Some people may say that I have had a very bad childhood or my childhood memories were not so great. There are always exceptional cases where situation cannot be controlled. It all depends on your destiny.

I can give you knowledge but if you can't interpret it properly then you are just left with half of what is thought to you. Similarly life does everything for us. Life teaches us lessons necessary for living the hard way, but if the lessons are not learnt properly we fall short in being happy in our journey and if we aren't able to understand lessons of life then we live a false life, as we struggle to find happiness.

The reason I mentioned all these questions related to your childhood was to guide your path towards your core memory which has been stored in your subconscious mind and it would be there for life.

Why are these childhood memories so important that they are stored for life?

All these childhood memories have an impact over our Adult behavior, character and responsibilities.

All these memories are called core memories which come together and develop into our personality. In other simple words what you are today is because of your childhood core memories. Your current behavior is due to your childhood nature. The seeds of your life which you live now were sown in your childhood. Whatever your perceptions are today is based on your childhood experiences.

80% of your brain gets developed before you turned 5 years of age. Whatever you learn during this time helps you building your personality.

Apart from your personality whatever experiences you gain in your childhood may it be good or may it be bad, consequences from both are remembered throughout our life. For example as children, whenever we used to do mischief or do something wrong we used to be punished by our parents.

Punishments are given to us in order to promote right behavior which helps us being a better person in life. This is the first principle we learn about life. We need to understand life by these small punishments we get, by doing so we learn to differentiate between right and wrong/good or bad.

When life gives us punishments we feel bad about the idea of being punished and we start cribbing about it, as punishment takes away our freedom.

Always remember one thing

'It is our false self called EGO which makes us believe negative, when it is POSITIVE'

- Mahesh Chandnani

EGO is described by me as evil governing over. I believe that there are two different personalities inside us one good and one bad. These two different personalities are present in every human being as we have an Angel inside us and we also have a devil inside us. We are like a coin which has two different sides one being good and the other being bad. Only one side of a coin is seen at a time similarly only one avatar of our personality is seen at a time. We can either be good or be bad. We can't portrait these two different parts of our personality in one single time. So when we behave well in our life we have our ANGEL side which is governing us that time. This makes us behave kind to people. Similarly when we behave rude to people it is our DEVIL side that takes over causing the **E**VIL to **GOVERN OVER**. This is what EGO stands for and that is why it is the most harmful thing for all humans. It is like cancer to our personality. EGO is self caused and only we can control it. Cancer can be controlled by medication but EGO doesn't have any medications. The evil side in us can be only controlled by our ANGEL side within.

As we go ahead with this book I will explain you how this EGO can be completely taken under control and stop its interference from our daily life.

What EGO does to us it that it says 'I am the most superior amongst all and how can something else over power me'. Nobody in this world likes to be dominated by any other person or things. It is the EGO in us which starts disrespecting the person who punishes us for our own brighter future. We never realize what our bigger picture looks like but we start hating our parents and teachers for punishing us. The most anger and disrespect is shown to GOD, who is blamed for everything when things go wrong in our life. We all have ups and downs in our life but we can't blame anybody else apart from our own self as we are solely responsible for all that happens in our life.

Let me give an oldest example from the famous story of ADAM AND EVE.

ADAM was the first human being god had created to live on this beautiful world. God was so happy by creating ADAM that he called all his angels to bow down to ADAM as he was his best creation so far. One of the angels called SATAN didn't like idea to bow down to ADAM. SATAN refused to bow down to a CREATION OF GOD which was created after him. According to SATAN, ADAM was inferior to him and he shall not bow down to ADAM. GOD didn't like the behavior of SATAN and he dismissed him from the heavens above to deepest part below the earth. ADAM was told to live on this planet earth enjoying all that is available for him but god had stopped ADAM from touching the tree of wisdom and had strictly warned him not to eat its fruits. Being the only one present on earth ADAM felt the need of a companion. GOD took ADAM'S one rib and made another one of a kind creation for ADAM. ADAM saw GOD had created WOMAN for him. He was happy looking at her as she was created from his RIB. ADAM called this woman EVE, ADAM and EVE were the first couple on this earth which lived happily until the day when SATAN came to EVE. SATAN knew that he could not affect ADAM as he was one of the finest creations of GOD but he thought if he could somehow convince EVE to ask ADAM to eat the fruit from the wisdom tree he could take the revenge from GOD by putting ADAM in trouble. SATAN came to eve asking for her to eat the apple from the wisdom tree it was the angel side of EVE that didn't want to listen to SATAN. EVE was not in the favor of doing this as she knew GOD had stopped them from eating the fruit of the wisdom tree. SATAN kept on trying until he gave birth to Evil side within EVE by saying that 'once you eat the apple from the wisdom tree you would no longer be requiring GOD as your Master. It is god who has stopped you from having the fruit of wisdom as he wants to keep all the powers for himself alone. God never wants to see you both be like him that is why he has stopped you both from eating that fruit'. EVE was convinced with the EVIL idea of overpowering GOD. This was the time when EGO was born. The EVIL side of EVE had started governing over her senses making her go to ADAM and force him to eat the fruit from the wisdom tree as she wanted ADAM to be as powerful as GOD who was the creator of them. ADAM who didn't want to do this tried each and every way possible to explain EVE why we shouldn't disrespect our creator but the Evil side Governing Over EVE did not want to hear a NO from him. ADAM losing all the arguments with EVE, he had to listen to her as she was created for him and he didn't want to lose her companionship. ADAM was finally convinced.

The Apple from the wisdom tree was eaten by ADAM for EVE but there was no explanation left to be given to GOD. As in the eyes of GOD ADAM had broken the trust between ADAM and him. CREATOR had lost in front of the EVIL causing ADAM to make mistake that has caused sufferings for humanity.

No matter what the circumstances are once a mistake is committed it always affects our life. One has to be punished over the sins as it shall get the lesson of not repeating it again. That is why we see good times and bad times in life. Good once are the results of good deeds we do in life and bad times are the result of bad behaviors committed by us.

This concept of good and bad is more beautifully explained by word KARMA. KARMA states that what deed we do, it may be a good deed or a bad deed it always comes back to us in multiplied forms of it. For example if we do good we get great in return but if we do bad then we may expect worst things in return. The reason I am explaining KARMA to you is because we keep on doing good deeds and bad deeds all our lives but we fail to understand why Bad things happen to us in our life. You may think how it would be possible for us to remember. We cannot remember each and every good or bad deed done by us. The truth is whatever you have been doing or have done up till now has resulted in your current life. The problems we are facing now in our current life are because of our bad deeds.

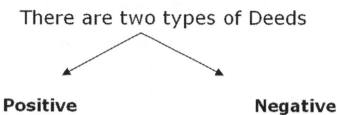

When I talk about positive deeds I mean to say is the good karmas you have conducted which have resulted in bringing happiness for others. Other type of deed is called negative deed it is a bad karma done by causing harm to others.

It is all categorized by how we treat other people around us. Are we good to them or are we bad to them. Have we ever hurt anyone deliberately? It is really important to know if this kind of behavior is present within our personality. We need to know this because we need to first fix what is wrong in our life and then think about building dreams on it. Our childhood again plays a big role in building such kind of good or bad personality of our life.

"Destiny has everything we want from it but it depends on what we are searching for in life"

- Mahesh Chandnani

If we lived in a negative surrounding or have had a lot of negative memories from past we would not be in a search of happiness as our happiness would be obstructed by negative thoughts based on our previous negative experiences in life. The bad memories which we have lived were result of bad deeds. The thing we want to take from our bad memory is not the memory but the lesson we have learned from it. Punishments are given to us so that we become a better person ahead in life similarly we have to go through bad phases of life in order to learn life lessons which would help us develop into a better person in our future. For example if you are going through a bad phase of life, you are unhappy, not satisfied and need your answers, in this process you lose faith in GOD. All we do throughout the day is crib about life, trying to get out of this mess we get stuck between two walls one of sadness another of misery. Walking all the way between these walls we finally reach a point where you want to give up the fight. You want to stop doing what you have been doing all your life and give up as the **results of your efforts have never been desirable**. This is the time when you behave most positive in your life.

Let me explain you how. If you are thirsty and I give you a glass full of water to drink, you would be able to drink it properly without any difficulty. But in this same scenario if I add a pinch of chili powder in your glass full of water you would yet be able to drink it unknowing the fact that it contains chili powder. But You would stop drinking when the chili hurts you because you are thirsty you would again try to drink the same chili water, this time with all efforts you would finish 75% of the water present in the glass but would stop as your eyes are watering, your throat is burning and now you are demanding more water. This time when you see the chili water in your hand it has more of chilies in it and less of water as the chili powder has accumulated at the bottom. Now you have two options to choose from. Either you finish the drink that I have given you or leave it and find other sources of water to drink. If you select the second option then you are free to choose from many other sources that can be made available to you when you start searching for them. If you select the first option then you will have to drink the water full of chilies knowing the fact that it would cost you lot of problems after drinking it. If this same scenario was given to you what would you choose from the above given options It is easy to choose the option of leaving the glass as it is mentioned in this book but in real life when we go through the same scenario and we have to choose from two options which are either to continue what you have been doing or leave and opt for new possibilities, we always choose to continue with what we have been doing as it is comfortable to do so then exploring other new things in our life. **There are many other worst situations then drinking chili water in our life and these situations are attached with human emotions.**

Remember human emotions attached with situation of life =
memory stored in our subconscious mind. (Refer to page No.8)

These memories pop up in our conscious mind during the difficult times of our life. Making us aware about what had happened previously in similar kind of situation. Our conscious mind then stops us from taking any new decision as there is the emotion of fear that has affected our mind. If you would have drank the remaining chili water you would have continued your share of suffering as you would have decided not to do something you haven't done before. That is not giving up and choosing for something else which can be better. This is a true fact for millions of people who live spending their whole life in pain and suffering. These people have become so used to suffering that the desire of doing something new has vanished from for them within. Such people spend their lives complaining about how bad their life is but they would never do anything special to change their way of living. These people have become addicted to suffering. Negativity around them makes them crave for more negativity. That is why when you choose to not drink that chili water I called you the most positive as you choose to open doors to million other possibilities in life. It requires courage to bang open the door full of opportunities which has been kept shut all our life. The door of opportunity has been always present but it was our mind which never saw it.

"It is we who fail to find an alternative for our life's suffering"

- Mahesh Chandnani

Memories which come up to our conscious mind during bad times of life causing emotion of fear taking over our mind are just memories of bad experiences which have been created long back and are now stored inside our subconscious mind.

A new memory can be created with our courageous efforts. This can replace the old memory which is stored in our subconscious mind with the new one.

So we have to replace a bad emotion with a good emotion to make a new memory.

Negative emotion →positive emotion

Fear→Anticipation

Anger→ Calmness

Sadness→Happiness

Envy→Confidence

Enmity→Trust

Cruelty→Kindness

Expectation→Surprise

Hate→Love

Dislike →like

If you do not like something in your life you can change that thing by creating a new memory.

Then why not change all our bad memories from our past and create all new good memories redefining our character and upgrading our life.

The new you will get a new way to explore same old situations that have given you problems in life. All these bad memories of ours were witnessed by negative emotions earlier, this is the reason why we feel bad about our life. Life has never told us to feel BAD about it. It is we who needs to change our perspective about bad things in life. This upgrade would help us regain the control over EMOTIONAL SELF, making us feel positive about all the things we have in our life.

We learn a lot from our childhood experiences that is why we develop a defense mechanism against all the bad memories that have caused us problems.

This exercise will help you get rid of all your negative experiences stored as a memory in your subconscious mind since the beginning of your life.

No matter if you feel stupid writing down things that have given you bad experiences but writing down the Negative emotions stored within will help you change your perspective towards them. This in return would help you create a positive mindset.

You can keep this list for future references or can throw the list away keeping the positives with you.

SR NO	NEGATIVE EXPERIENCES	LESSONS LERNT	POSITIVE CONERSIONS
1)	My friend did not invite to his party.	You should not expect things from others	I will invite him to my party unlike him.
2)	I lied to my father	I feel guilty won't lie to my father again	I should have told him the truth and not lied
3)			
4)			
5)			
6)			
7)			

You need to write down more such experiences recollecting smallest things of your life that has been stored as a negative memory in your subconscious mind. Close your eyes and think about memories which have made you sad or feel bad in your childhood. Write them all down.

Now that you have come to know what is wrong in your life and how can you change your perspective from negative to positive memories. You have come to know the secret of changing a bad emotion into a good emotion, may it be any situation you can easily change your core memory that has been causing problems for you in your life.

There are a lot of things that you first need to understand in order to make a perfect change in your perspectives. This was just the beginning where you learnt about how your subconscious mind works and how an experience attached with human emotions becomes a memory. You have learnt the basics which will help you understand this entire philosophy of achieving things in life.

This first technique of changing your bad experience into good experiences will lead to know more about yourself. This is a life changing moment for you as things you are now going to learn will never be thought to you anywhere else. Life created by us becomes a complicated process of living, it's continues monotony full of problems.

"To understand your life you first need to KNOW WHO YOU ARE"

- Mahesh Chandnani

REDISCOVER THE CHILD IN YOU

"You are born for a special purpose in life you just need to understand your BEING and help others know theirs in life"

- Mahesh Chandnani

Rediscover The Child In You

We have learned in previous chapter about our life being directly influenced by our past memories. Our personality being a direct reflection of what we have learnt in our GOLDEN years of life known as CHILDHOOD.

This is how we learn things in life.

Stages	Years	Learnt from	%
Stage I	1-5	From parents	40%
Stage II	5-10	From teachers	5%
Stage III	10-15	From friends	25%
Stage IV	15-20	Analyzing Self	15%
Stage V	20 - 25	Inner bonding	5%

This chart shows us how an individual learns from different atmosphere grasping all the memories.

Based on these memoires an individual develops a unique personality which is portrayed in front of the world for the rest of his life. Every individual in this world goes from this leaning process in his life. Maximum amount of our personality comes from the first learning stage which is from our parents. We learn nearly **40%** of what we are today within first five years of our life. First five years of our life are most sensitive for us, as this period develops into 40% of our personality. You might have heard about the list of do's and don'ts in front of the children below the age of 5. Every generations of our family follows this list of do's and don'ts blindly without even understand why. Elders of our family always knew this and this knowledge was given to them from their elders and same goes for them. The thing is we sometimes do not even have time to think why we are doing something as following instructions are more comfortable than finding out the reason why one should not. We prefer learning from others experiences as it can be more dependable then learning from our mistakes.

When we were born to our parents it was they who thought us how to trust any other human being as it was them whom we first trusted our lives upon. After trust we learn many other things from them these things are as follows, how to crawl, how to eat, how to talk, how to walk, how to cycle, how to behave, how to be who you are, how to obey, how to respect, how to read, how to write, how to play, how to enjoy life, how to make friends in life, etc.

Parents are our first teachers in life. We grow learning all these things from our parents and other family members until we reach five years of our age and are ready to enter the second stage, which is going to school and learning from teachers.

School is the place where we spend more than 10 years of our life learning things about the world around us. What is thought in school by teachers during the age 5 to 10 is used by us in our day to day life. Second stage of learning teaches us useful things that we would be utilizing throughout our life. Learning languages and basic mathematics is most commonly remembered from this stage in life. The major different from stage one and stage two is that in stage one of learning we are given personal attention by our parents while they teach us important lessons that are necessary for living. While in school we are generally thought about important things in a group having 40+

students. This is why we only learn **5%** of our personality from our teachers as it is not personally thought.

Third stage of life brings more variety of learning. The experiences we get in this third stage of learning are divided into two different parts. We will discuss two different aspects of it in detail later but first we need to understand third stage of learning. Stage one was pure learning, in stage two we understood the world around us but when we enter stage three we are completely stranger to it.

What we had first learnt in life was to trust other people around us and this emotion of trust is tested the most in this third stage of learning. We start sharing our world with a lot of same age people we call friends. Some friends we make are elder to us, while some are younger to us, rest are same aged. We call such people friends because this is the first time in life when we learn to trust someone else apart from our family members. Learning to trust them makes us to start sharing our life with them.

There are a lot of things happening in our life in the stage three of learning. We are exploring new set of views, understanding other people's Ideas and sharing our own individual perspectives to the world. We learn who we are, how much knowledge we have and how much more we need to grow, etc. It is a clear stage of exploration where we have the freedom to choose whom we want to have as our friends, what communities we want to spend time with and what things we want to share with friends. We also come to know about our personality which we have developed since past 10 to 12 years of living. There is a lot of comparison which starts from this stage of learning. The compression takes place between you and others. You may yourself want to know how good you are compared to other individuals around you. How fast you can make friends with people around you or there are some mistakes you are doing, that people are choosing not to be friends with you.

Friends are an important phase of your life as they score second highest influencing your personality. After your parents teach you how to live in this society, our teachers teaches us what is required to live in this society. But it is friends that teach you more about who you are and what you want to be.

You learn about yourself for the first time
from other people's point of you.

When you are in this third stage of learning, you learn how you are respected by your friends, how they care for you, how they like to talk to you, how they share their ideas with you, etc but with all this we also see the dark side of friendship which is, what they don't like about you, how they always judge you, you are criticized for sharing your opinions, insulted or made fun of just for their entertainment, what happens when they do not like something about you, where they consider you wrong, and the worst to see is how they can behave when you do not do something for them.

Life becomes a survival game for you as you need to be good to your friends and obey them to be part of their group. It's a continues struggle in life where you keep on doing what they say forgetting what you have learnt in the first two stages of life. You keep on changing yourself, from one group to another. Finally there comes a time when we are left with no friends as people whom we have spent changing ourselves for, stops recognizing us because we have been paying so much of attention to what they would think about us. This has made us lost our own identity. This truly happens in teenage as we are mostly around with friends in this age. Another scenario is where you absolutely do not have friends and this loneliness makes you wanting to change the way you are so that you can make friends and experience what is friendship.

So either you have friends or you do not have friends, you learn many new things about yourself. Whatever you have learnt from your first and the second stage of learning is put to test in the third stage of learning.

The third stage of learning has two parts

1) Friends
2) Puberty

Apart from friends in the third stage of learning we come across something really different. It is a major change within our body called **PUBERTY.** Puberty is one of the major reasons why, things change in our life during the third stage of learning. It teaches us more than what our friends might have thought us. Having friends is important, what they think about us is more important but what kind of relationship we share with them is the most important factor which is thought to us by puberty.

We learn **25%** of our personality from this third stage of learning out of which 10% comes from our friends while the other 15% comes from puberty. Puberty is not just about physical changes that happen to our body it has a lot more than that. PUBERTY changes the way we think, it gives us the capacity to understand more complex mechanisms that becomes a part of our body during this stage. The hormonal changes lead to mood fluctuations causing us to have mixed emotions at times.

Puberty is inevitable. It is not something we choose but is something that happens to every individual. May it be a girl or may it be a boy everyone goes through Puberty in the third stage of learning. Many girls start with puberty in their second stage of learning while for boys it always starts in the third stage of learning. We learn a lot from friends, we understand their perspective but our relationship with them is guided by puberty. It is Puberty that makes us aware about our likes and dislikes, making us choose whom we want to be with and whom we would not want to be with.

Our general life which was first lived according to other people perspective now becomes more specific for us. This helps us dealing with emotional matters. There are now close friends whom we want to spend more time with then other friends. We learn to differentiate close friends and acquaintances. We become mature and learn to choose friends, whom we can be ourselves with.

Such friends we make in this stage become like family for us, as it is after the first stage that we have chosen few bunch of people with whom we can be ourselves as we be with our family.

It all starts when you become friends with other kids being of your age, you start talking about common things between you both share followed by the uncommonness which makes you both become best friends as you both know common as well as uncommon things between your lives. At this stage you can choose to be best friends like you both are or become more close friends.

This happens when you both are familiar with the differences as well as the common factors between you both and are ready to respect them as they are. Not all best friends become close friends as it requires an important role one has to play for the other. A close friend can be even more important for you then your family members. As your close friend knows everything about you and accepts you the way you are also cares for you like your family. A small fight between your close friends can result in deepest pain for you during the time of puberty. This phase of life teaches us who our close friends are with whom we can share every little detail of our teenage life with. Right from who we are, what we do, whom we like or have a crush on, whom we hate, what food we eat, what we do when we are alone, what makes us comfortable, etc. Another aspect of life which comes in front of us during the time of puberty is **LOVE**. Puberty makes us learn what feelings are, why we find someone so special, whom we are so attracted to, what makes us nervous talking to them, how we fall in love, etc.

From friends —> best friends —> close friends —> love

This is how we learn to differentiate between other people apart from our family members in the third stage of learning. The emotion of love is most felt in the form of attraction by the opposite sex. Falling in love teaches many new things in life which has always been unaware to us as we experience this kind of emotion for the first time in life. That is why this third stage of learning dominates on our personality. As in this stage a lot of importance is given on others point of you, which results in affecting our true personality. The graph of learning and exploring new things in life comes down with the end of puberty. Puberty for some girls and guys ends with the end of third stage of learning. It is a very personal phenomenon that occurs differently for every individual so for some it ends in the third stage of learning while for others it ends in the fourth stage of learning in life.

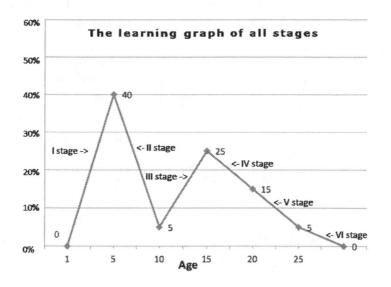

The learning graph of life

With the end of third stage of learning we are now pushed to fourth stage of learning where we have to choose from what we have learnt and what we want our personality to be, for the rest of our life.

This fourth stage of learning brings us close to our own self and makes us realize how we are, who we were and what we will be like in future. This future responsibility of being able to decide what we want to be known as in life is quite brilliantly timed by our destiny for us, as by this period of our life we have come to know ourselves better. Learning from all three stages of life we have now stepped into the shoes of maturity where our role now is to define our future. In this fourth stage of our learning we now have all the experiences learnt from three different stages of learning. These memories are stored in our subconscious mind.

Our destiny now gives us a chance to live a life based on our own desires we are now given freedom to choose what we want in our lives. All these years we have lived according to someone else for example in the first stage of learning we live our life according to our parents. In the second stage of life we live according to our teachers, in the third stage of life we have multiple influences in life coming from our friends, puberty and our love. But now in the fourth stage learning, life gives us a chance to summarize all that we have learnt from previous three stages, putting everything together it gives us a chance to solve our puzzled life.

"After puberty comes a sense of responsibility,
making us lead our life based on our wishes"

- Mahesh Chandnani

Many people face difficulties during this phase of life as they cannot resemble themselves from whom they used to be in the first two stage of learning and who they have become after third stage of learning. It is like homework, life wants us to do on the subject of our life. The question which the fourth stage of learning asks every individual is

What your life is going to be like in future?

It is in this stage where we decide our careers that we pursue for life. If we do not do our homework right we may end up destroying our lives. We can either make our future by researching about our own personality or can live the life in the complete darkness and continue living the same way for entire lifetime. Think about your life 5 years down the line from now, it can be what you want to create or it can just go to a completely opposite direction. Life we live in present is an impression of who we used to be, which is why to have a desired future with all that we want to achieve in our life, we needs to change many things of our present life. In this forth stage of learning, life gives us a chance to understand who we really are, when we were in our first stage of learning. Everything then was thought to us by our parents and we never questioned why they were teaching us all this? As the first thing we learnt from them was **Trusting**.

Trust is one thing that makes us live depending on someone in a completely strange environment. For example a new born baby learns to trust first the mother as the baby recognizes her most after the delivery, second the baby learns to trust his father followed by other family members. Trust is not something that is created by us but it is something that is felt within. Trust develops slowly by spending time and understanding others.

We trust our parents in the first stage of learning we trust our teachers in the second stage of learning. These two stages of learning are generally harmless for majority of children but the real trust issues that we experience in life comes from the third stage of learning. Trust is tested in this third stage of learning because we now learn to trust a person coming from totally different atmosphere, background and family. All our friends differ from each other because they have their different backgrounds and family to which they belong.

Our trust is broken many times in this phase of life. And it happens to us because we randomly trust our friends as our well wishers but we are often proven wrong by their wrong intensions. A broken trust memory is a bad experience which gets stored in our subconscious mind. This bad experience makes us a different person as we compare this bad experience of our life to all other experiences. Stopping ourselves from doing the same mistake again, we stop ourselves from exploring the new experiences which can be good.

This makes us loose trust in our own self as we always think bad consequences even before trying to explore what life has for us. Our mind becomes negative shattering our self esteem. We lose our confidence and are not able to decide what is good for us in life. Entering the fourth stage of learning we are lost in life. Without knowing anything about ourselves we just keep on living for the sake of it.

The third stage of learning makes us loose all our personality which we had made in the first two stages of learning. This happens to majority of us in our teenage as we lose our direction of life. We start living a life which is nothing else but a lie. This happens to us because we have lost trusting our own personality which we once use to do with pride. Think about it the first two stages of life they were always happily spend without any major kind of troubles caused. This was because we used to believe in ourselves before, which now we do not. Trusting our own identity is more important than trusting others in this society. It is our gut feeling first that makes us believe in what is right for us. If we are feeling bad about something it is we who will suffer in pain nobody else comes to help us during this struggle, we easily start believing in other peoples perspectives and start changing our identities according to their likes and dislikes. We mold our self into a complete new identity, while we do not ask for any changes in them. Our new self is lost with the person for whom we had changed causing us to become aloof with our own identity. Let me give you an example to be clear.

When you were at school there were all kind of students around you, some you liked to spend time with while others chose you to spend their time with. Groups are generally formed this way everywhere. To spend time with that group you want to be a part of, you used to alter your things, always adjusting to continue being a part of that same group. On the other hand there were other students who liked to spend time with you and would alter their lives according to your convenience in order to stay friends with you.

Life is all about this, we always run behind things that we are not. We fail to choose who we are, as it is our low self esteem that makes us the follower, while we can always choose becoming a **LEADER**. When you are following others perspective you are disrespecting who you are and this affects your identity as you continue to mold your personality. For you it is more important to catch up with others but less important to check whether what you are doing is making you develop into a completely new personality. This new personality is going to be very different from who you yourself used to be. When you give away the control of your life to another person you are making a mistake which is going to make you lose your identity for life, you will end up being a confused personality which would not be a good sign in the fourth stage of learning. People often do not like to be around a person who is not sure about his own believes.

If we do not know about our own self, how will we be able to portrait ourselves in front of others. This confused personality causes a lot of problems in our life. Earlier we were not sure of our destination but now we are unsure of our own identity. The question of what we want in our life becomes secondary as for now it is mandatory to resolve the problem of **WHO WE ARE**. You cannot determine your dreams in life if you're not aware of your own reality. It is important to REDISCOVER YOURSELF by finding THE CHILD IN YOU. This is the second thing we learn in the FORTH stage of learning.

It is all about self analysis that one needs to check in order to understand **WHO WE REALLY ARE.**

THREE STEPS WE HAVE TO LEARN IN THE FOURTH STAGE OF LEARNING	
FIRST STEP	SUMMARIZE ALL THREE STAGE OF LEARNING
SECOND STEP	REDISCOVER THE CHILD IN YOU
THIRD STEP	BE DAY DREAMER

Many people really forget who they really are in life after their third stage of learning as for them the third person point of view becomes very important as compared to their own personality. You may find yourself filled with such people's examples around you. These people are not true to themselves, they wear a mask of fakeness over their face. These kinds of people talk good in front of you but behind your back they are your worst enemies of your life.

The reason behind these people behaving this way is that they have adopted their personality from only their third stage of learning. It is revenge mechanism that drives such people to behave this way. This happens to them because when they were judged wrong by their friends and other people around during their third stage of learning they started believing in ways mentioned below.

What these people believe in different stages	
First stage of learning	I love my life
Second stage of learning	I m such a good being.
Third stage of learning	People make fun of me Am I really that bad?
Fourth stage of learning	I should make fun of people and criticize them before they do same to me.

They start living a life full of suffering. They believe that this is how life is going to be for them, these people start being bad with people as they think people also behave badly with them. Believing in this philosophy they surrender themselves to the world of evil and become a fake personality. They can never resemble who they used to be as they have changed themselves completely. There are another set of people who give up their personality as they no more can face this cruel world alone. These people do not become fake people as mentioned above but these people take up alcoholism as their final destination of life. Alcoholism makes these kind of people feel good about themselves and also helps them forget what other people think or say about such alcoholics. Alcoholism starts only in the fourth stage of learning. You will not see any person getting dependent on alcohol completely in first three stages of learning. You may find people consume alcohol in their third stage learning but that doesn't make them dependent of alcohol completely. This is why we need to perfectly develop our personality based on all three stages of learning. You cannot have your personality entirely based on anyone stage of learning that is first, second or third stage.

"The learning which you chose will determine the life you are going to live"

- Mahesh Chandnani

We learn **15%** of our personality from this fourth stage of learning. The personality which is destined for us is lost inside us and our job now is to find this hidden personality within. The reason why it is more important to recognize our true self is because when we know who we are then only we can determine what we want from our life. It takes you 18 years to learn about yourself completely.

In our childhood we never cared about what other person would think about our mischief or how others would judge us. As kids we always believed in our self. So to change all our negative experiences and bad emotions we again need to **REDISCOVER THAT CHILD IN US.**

Find the child who never cared about what others thought about him. The child who lived his life enjoying each day forgiving and forgetting all bad memories, the child who found happiness in smallest things. If this child is inside you then you have to find this child in order to solve all your problems in life. Let me show you how we can solve our problems in the next chapter.

**BE
DAY
DREAMER**

Adults → DREAMS

Teenage = Problems

Childhood ← solutions

-Mahesh Chandnani

Be Day Dreamer

In our life, we have been living a life based upon our past experiences. The person whom we think we are now is actually the result of past deeds. We dream about future but we always have our back facing at our dreams and we always live our life looking behind facing our past experiences. Whatever new situation comes in our present life we always have to look back to our past experiences in order to tackle these situations.

Let me give you an example which you can relate to easily. When you first fall in love or have your crush that you want to tell your feelings there is a fear within us that stops us for doing so and that fear is of REJECTION. We all go through this stage in our life, be it a guy or a girl we all have crushes and we are scared to talk to them because the fear makes us nervous in front of them. If you have ever approached someone in life then you may have felt the pinch of rejection in life this rejection makes us weak inside as whenever we encounter similar situation again in life we always tend to compare our previous experience with our present life. Doing this we either quit before trying or conclude negative as being rejected again.

**We always face the world of past experiences,
showing our back to our future dreams.**

While we have to learn to

**Turn your face to our future world of dreams,
leaving behind the lane of past experiences.**

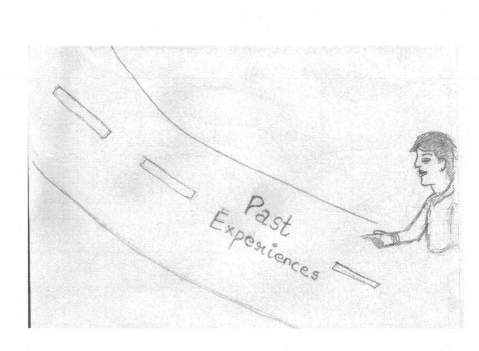

We always face our past experiences

We need to turn our face to the future world of dreams.

Our life is full of challenges and it is on us to decide whether we want to achieve success or give up our fight and surrender in front of them. When we turn our face towards our dreams we open our doors to a life which has been waiting for us all the time.

We forget all about our past and start living each day of our life as a new challenge. It is a life where we enjoy solving all the obstacles of our life. Having a smile on our face, we turn every page of our life. This is what we learn to do in the fourth stage of learning. Closing all the doors of our past we open our doors to ocean full of opportunities that makes us enjoy every day of our life. Our present life becomes a new present for us. We need to open the gift specially given to us by GOD.

"To find happiness in your daily life, you will have to everyday live your life like GOD'S PRESENT TO YOU"

- Mahesh Chandnani

Majority of our daily problems are created by us because of our habit of comparing every new situation with our past experiences. It is our daily practice which leads us to do such a thing all the time. It is a bad habit in us which can be cured by deliberately inculcating a good habit into practice.

A habit is nothing else but an experience we store in our subconscious mind, an experience which we practice daily with our conscious efforts and later is carried by our subconscious mind automatically. When we turn our face towards the unknown life ahead, it is the notion of adventure that strikes from within. All of a sudden we feel courageous in life as if we were born for this enlightenment. This notion makes us be who we are or in other words, whom we were born (destined) to be. The real meaning of life is understood by us in the fourth stage of learning. People who fail to understand this enlightenment struggle in darkness throughout their lives.

Gautama Buddha said **life is full of suffering.** Indeed it is, we suffer throughout our life there is emotional stress all the time in our life but there is hope for all human beings to survive. Hope is the sign of positivity one has in this negative world. Hope for us is like a ray of light that is going to take us away from darkness. This hope for us is this fourth stage of learning that enters in our dark life showing us the path that can lead us to find happiness in our life. You will learn how to be happy in every situation? What happiness actually means in our life? Where to find happiness in our life? And many more questions about happiness in more detail in the next chapter **UPGRADE FOR HAPPINESS** but before we learn about happiness, we first need to open our doors to the world of Imagination the word imagination is deeply connected to our golden era of life called childhood.

Every child has the power to create his own WORLD

When we are kids we always are running after new things in life, the more we explore as children the less it seems to our imagination. For example when we were young we used to learn many new things from different sources in life. When we had learned that birds can fly we used to stretch our arms out and run as fast as we can, we imagined ourselves flying in the air like the birds fly. Another example, looking at people drive a car we would as children hold up to any round shaped thing available and would start rotating it, imagining ourselves as driving a car holding round shaped steering wheel.

There are many such examples we can relate to from our childhood with context of our imagination. This is even more relevant when it comes to our future professions, we all have had a list of various professions we imagined doing in our future life. In our childhood we used to learn things by looking at people, when we used to visit doctors we used to grasp how they are. When we used to go to school we used grasp how teachers are, similarly we used to grasp many such people in the first two stages of learning. Grasping all such professions we used then imagine being one of them in our future.

This power of imagination was a key to our happiness but this imaginary world gets lost in the third stage of learning. In this unfortunate third stage of learning we only learn to think about what is and what is not but never imagine what it can be. Our perceptions in life become so realistic that our skill of imaginations comes to a halt.

Our future slowly keeps on diminishing as the pressure of reality keeps on increasing. We are now left with no time for ourselves. All day we spend in school, homework, friends, television or the latest trend, all over the world is using Smartphone, etc.

We carry this same all day busy lifestyle to our fourth stage of learning, without having time for our own selves we spend our life living for others. That is why imagination for us is really important we cannot just judge our life by seeing one side of it, our life has a lot more for us and it is our responsibility to choose what we want from it.

People use LAW OF ATTRACTION to attract things in their life. Thinking that they have become like magicians as they are able to create what they want in life. The real truth about law of attraction is that these people just attract who they are and not what they want from life. Let me show an example.

People confuse themselves between their imaginative powers and their boring reality. When it comes to manifest a brand new car you want to buy for yourself this Christmas, you first need to decide what model you wish to buy, the real deal is if you want to create this car in your life buy using LAW OF ATTRACTION, then you need to be really specific about your future. What we do is that we confuse our selves by changing the cars we want, the worst scenario is when people talk about buying new cars but always say that 'I m happy with the car I have right now it is not giving me troubles' so should I really buy the car I want. These things would seem funny to you now but we all stuck ourselves in such situations daily. If you are happy with what you have then what is the need to confuse yourself by attracting something that you already have. This is a contradiction that takes place between world of imagination and the world of reality. Our reality is just created by our past imaginations. Who you are today is the result of what you thought about being yesterday. So if you consider yourself happy with what you have in your reality then why you keep on crying and cribbing about your life being not satisfactory. Law of attraction is one more step in the stage four of learning that makes us closer in knowing ourselves.

"A **DREAM** is a GATEWAY to Get Rid of ALL Your Problems"

- Mahesh Chandnani

When you were a child you used to cry for chocolates or ice cream in front of your parents. They world in return give you, what you want as they want to see you happy. Similarly when we grow elder in life and are in our stage four of learning we have to struggle for getting things in life and this time parents tell us to take our own responsibility. We do not cry for things now and even if we do cry it is on an emotional level. Crying in front of parents at this age is considered being immature in our society. But cribbing about things is sure a mature thing. Crying is now converted into cribbing for things, which leads our life to unhappiness. Like crying being one of our childhood habits we have many other habits from our childhood stored within us. So why not focus of the habit of imagination and learn to explore our life in a new way, making it our everyday routine.

Imagination as children wasn't really important but achieving things now is our first criteria in life. In this comparative and competitive world we want to show people what we are capable of doing. The real question that we wonder in this fourth stage of learning is that do we really know what exactly we are searching for in this life. We have been struggling to know ourselves since 18 to 19 years of living but are yet unaware of our true desires. Law of attraction is a technique that helps you desire as many things you want in your life, but only manifests things which we desire from within. Law of attraction makes us become DAY DREAMER. This technique has a lot to do with what is within you but many people all over the world fail to realize this. We keep on focusing to create what we want in life but fail to understand why we are creating it. We use Law of attraction to create good for us but what really happens is we end creating bad things for us. This happens because we are not clear about things we want and why we want them.

Let me give you an example from my life where I used Law of attraction unknowingly that created a problem and this happened to me cause of my unclear ideas, resulting to suffer consequences.

When I was in my 12th grade in high school, I used to be part of many extracurricular activities. I would always like to volunteer myself for majority of events because I liked to organize them. I was an average student when it came to academic but I would always be an active member in the events committee, this made me popular among students. During this time of life, I always used to attract being popular among the college staff and faculty members. I wanted to be known by them as well.

"GREED is and unwanted motive of life that CREATES PROBLEMS"

- Mahesh Chandnani

Being an average student I used to always see scholars getting attention from principal and other staff members, while I also wanted that attention and it was little difficult to get it from academics.

Knowing the technique of attraction I started applying steps required to attract what you desire. Days went by and months went by I kept on attracting this desire which stated 'something should suddenly happen, that example of mine should be given to my fellow students making me famous among the teachers and faculty member'.

Nothing really happened and I gave up the idea of attracting it as it wasn't helping me. Soon came the time of our exams and everyone started preparing for our internal submissions. Unfortunately during this period of time I was diagnosed with MALARIA. Malaria is kind of fever that is caused by the bite of female anopheles mosquitoes. I had suffered from malaria many times in life but this time it had caused me a lot of weakness. This weakness has made me stay at home for a lot of time making me give up on my internal exams. My mom had visited my high school asking them to allow me to give my exam separately. On medical terms I was allowed to sit for my internal exams on a separate day that was specially arranged for me. I had to give all my internal submission on this day. You may be wondering that I had got what I had attracted for but no there is more to the story. After submitting the internals I got an ample amount of time to rest and prepare myself for my final exams. I gave my exams well, everything went fine. We get three months of summer vacations after our exams. I had a fun time with friends during this summer time passed and even vacations came to an end. All we waited now was for our results to come out. When online results showed up my name wasn't there in the list, it was very disappointing for me, I called up my high school but they said the mark sheets haven't come yet and I will have to wait for the mark sheets to come. I waited for ten more days thinking about what could have gone wrong. After ten days came our mark sheet you will not believe what had happened. I was called to meet the vice principal without knowing anything I had gone to meet her. The first thing they did was gave me my mark sheet. To me everything seemed fine in it, I had scored well in all the papers but yet the results showed fail, entire staff was amazed with this kind or mark sheet I had got from the university as it was first time something like this had happened. What actually went wrong was created by my daily process of using Law of attraction to become popular amongst teachers and faculty members never knew something so big can be created causing me to suffer this consequence.

Yet thinking what went wrong? Let me answer that question for you. The reason why my result showed fail was because me being marked as ABSENT for the paper of environmental studies. When the office staff found out the reason how this had happened, it was hilarious for me. During the time of internal submissions, our Environmental studies teacher had gone on a maternity leave. All the responsibility of distributing the marks was handed over to various other teachers from the staff. When the special day was selected for me because of my illness the office had informed all the teachers to take my test on that particular day for me and because our Environmental studies teacher was on leave there was no one to take my EVS internals. when I went to college that day I gave all the tests but due to my illness i wanted to finish as soon as I can and reach home to rest, we didn't realized the absence of EVS teacher and nobody else cared about this. Even though office staff had given the responsibilty for handling EVS marks to other respective teachers, they didn't bother in confirming why I had been absent on the internal submission day. When the marks were being sent to the university the teacher responsible for marks nicely marked me ABSENT on the place where the marks were supposed to be written. This ABSENT came on my mark sheet which resulted as Fail, even after of doing my responsibility of letting the staff know the reason of me not being able to submit my internals on the time and even they agreeing to arrange a special day for me. Due to the EVS teacher being on leave this whole situation was created. I had to reappear my Environmental studies (EVS) exam just to clear my internals, this process made me waste a year of education. All I am trying to portrait is that if you do not know what you are attracting and how it is going to affect you in your life, you should not really put in efforts to attracting something that can give you problems for life. This happens only when we start attracting things without knowing our own selves.

"Know WHO YOU ARE to ATTRACT best in life"

- Mahesh Chandnani

I would have saved a year of education if I wouldn't have attracted this in life. It was my greed for fame which made me desperate in being known by the office staff teachers and the principal. This was given to me multiplied, what I wanted was them to give my example to other students and guess what, when the results were given to students in the auditorium, our principal announced my name giving my example of how a student can fail if they do not submit their internals on time. My example is till date given to thousands of students who appear for XII grade from that high school.

LAW OF ATTRACTION gives you what you want, without knowing the fact that how it is going to affect you or how you will suffer the consequences. It is a give and take situation where if you are asking for something there has to be someone who has to give it to you. Whatever it is in our life we have asked for is given to us by someone or the other, Vice versa. We cannot say that we had not attracted something like this and we wanted something else. Law of attraction does not have a brain to understand like we do, that is why we are always asked to be specific when using this law. Knowingly or unknowingly we attract things in our life may it be good or may it be bad it is given to us because we have attracted it in our life. think about it in my case, my teacher went on maternity leave, I was down with malaria, nobody else was affected with her absence but it was me who had to suffer this consequence as I was solely responsible for creating this whole confusion because I had deliberately demanded to be famous among the faculty and teachers, not only this but I had even asked for my example to be given to all other students. It wasn't small thing to ask for, I had asked for something that had to be specially created for me. And it worked perfectly fine. I couldn't understand how it had happen then but later in life I realized that it was all created by me.

I was able to create this using the power of Attraction, without knowing the need of why I wanting it, I created something which was totally unwanted in life. Imagine if I knew myself completely then and I had calculated what I really wanted in life. What I would then create would be best of what I really wanted rather than wasting power on something which was not required in life.

If I tell you to attract money in your life you won't be able to successfully do so because your thoughts will always doubt yourself owning that much amount of money in your life. This happens because we just want to attract money materially without having an essence of owning it in life. This is what blocks us in making our dreams come true. The problem is not in achieving but the problem lies within, we forget who we are while attracting what we are not, which is why our manifestations doesn't always match to our desires and we end up living the same life we used to live all our life.

The fourth stage of learning allows you to know yourself within giving you the capability to compare your thoughts with your present life called <u>REALITY</u> this is the time when you learn how to attract what you want in your life properly. If you attract things properly you will be able to attract money but if think about just surviving then won't be able to. Your dream is to attract money but your thoughts are about surviving. You are contradicting yourself and the process does not match, if you need to attract money you need to be one with the thoughts you feel. This would result the attracted thing in being part of you, making your imagination work wonders for you. Let me explain you how it is done. Imagine yourself being RICH. Now take one step ahead of imagination and feel the essence of being rich. To know the essence of being rich you will have to research on rich people in the sense, how they be, what they do, what they wear, how they talk, what style they carry, whom they are friends with, every little things matters to us about them. We need to learn how they live their life and specially the art of multiplying their money. Money isn't the only aspect of living we have many other desires we wish to achieve in our journey of life. Law of attraction helps us in the fourth stage of learning to develop a more ambitious way of life. It reflects our thoughts, making us proud of being ourselves. The very person whom you did not wanted to be in the third stage of learning, you have starting loving yourself in the fourth stage of leaning as you have learnt to be DAY DREAMER.

Being a day dreamer makes us the person who can dream about anything he wants in his life and with efforts of understanding himself he can then calculate the pros and cons involved in attracting that particular thing in his or her life. Day dreaming teaches you, how much energy you can put in daily to achieve something you really want in your life. But it is important to know why you want to achieve it as if you do not know the reason behind achieving then it can cause you the consequences.

Practicing only law of attraction can often lead you to a path of greediness, which makes a person so attached to the thing he wants to attract and if he is not able to get that thing in his life, he makes his life miserable by thinking negative about his life. He blames the whole process of law of attraction responsible for his failure in life as he has been stuck on that one thing that wasn't granted to him. This kind of behavior is only experienced by some towards the end of their fourth stage of learning.

We learn 15% of our personality in stage four of learning. We develop 5% of our personality by summarizing our FIRST THREE STAGES OF LEARNING. The second 5% comes from REDISCOVERING THE CHILD IN US and the third 5% comes from learning the Law of attraction that makes us BE A DAY DREAMER in life. Being a Day Dreamer in life gives us an opportunity to dream about thinks we want in our life daily, but what it also does is makes us carried away in attracting unwanted things in life. In order to learn more about how you can attract things in life knowing the difference between 'attracting in need' and 'attracting in greed' you will have to understand how you can **upgrade for happiness** in life. We attract things that make us happy, so why not upgrade our life for happiness. I will teach you how you can **UPGRADE FOR HAPPINESS** in the next chapter.

> **"Every individual has the power to change their capabilities to develop 'WHAT IS' and 'WHAT IT CAN BE' in their life."**

> - **Mahesh Chandnani**

UPGRADE FOR HAPPINESS

"Problems, bad moods, frustrations, etc are just thoughts you allow to rest for a longer period of time in your mind"

- Mahesh Chandnani

Upgrade For Happiness

Stage four of learning thought us many new things in life. It gave us the ability to get rid of your past experiences and stay focused on every new day of life. It also thought us to use law of attraction to bring enthusiasm back in your life, that makes you keep a positive attitude in life and helps you develop a habit of attract good things in your life. But towards the end of the fourth stage of learning we find negativity sinking back. The reason we start getting negative in life again is because of our human mind. Our human mind is functioned to ask the question **WHY?,** for every situation in our life.

Let me explain you this with help of an example. When we first get up in the morning we are fully charged up with the energy which makes us excited about our day, with fresh thoughts in our mind we start our day every morning and we start feeling nice about our life. Everything is nice about our life until afternoon arrives, after lunch in the afternoon you start feeling a bit uneasy as your charged up mood which you had in the morning has started diminishing, this makes you feel dull and boring about your day. This is the time when your mind starts questioning you **WHY?** why do I have to work or attend lectures?, why can't I be at home all day?, why cannot I sleep on my bed right now? Why why why why why why why why, etc. our mind gives up finding answers to all such questions as for the mind what was in morning has now changed in the afternoon. This is the reason why coffees and teas were invented by humans and they became so important in the our lifestyle. It is a common thing throughout the world to consume coffee or tea daily in the late afternoon. Drinking coffee or tea recharges our self, making us remember the charge we had in the morning. It makes us feel fresh as we recollect our morning mood and try to create the same to remain charged up till night, by this example I m trying to show you what we had in the morning fades away by afternoon and we have to recollect it every evening so that we survive until we go to sleep at night. This may be little hard to understand but it is really important to know the reason behind the whole confusion. What we feel in the morning is the freshness that is the gift of nature given to us by the process of sleeping. We sleep 6 to 8 hours daily at night but what we try to recreate in the evening is the manual efforts of human beings as we try to create something which is not in our hands. You will understand more about nature and Energy that makes us fresh in the morning in this as well as the next chapter of this book. Before we know that we first need to understand the human mind and its ability to ask the question WHY? Human beings are the social animal, we all know this fact about human evolution and we have also studied how man has evolved from ancient times in our school. In the journey from apes to humans, our mind has developed an ability of reasoning that differentiates between the human brain and the animal brain. Reasoning is a process of thinking about something in a logical context. It is an ability of our mind which allows us to think and understand. This is why we humans have being progressing rapidly as our mind always asks the question WHY? And in the search of an answer our mind always leads to have unique observations, formulating something innovative which is new to the world. Imagine how our life would have been if our mind wouldn't have been able to think or ask the question why?, we wouldn't have developed as we have, there wouldn't have been any technology, no science nothing. Eat, sleep and survive have been the only thing we would have done our whole life. When we learnt law of attraction in life we learnt to attract new things that make us happy in our life. Law of attraction is brilliant thing that happens to us as it gives us dreams to be achieved in life. Every day we start following the steps which are required to be followed to make your dreams come true. First step of law of attraction is to believe in your own self that you would be capable enough to achieve it. Second step after believe, is to achieve, we need to believe in our life that what we desire in life has been already achieved by us. This step brings us closer in knowing our self accurately as we practice of achieving something that is not there in present but it has been already achieved in our mind. For example if you want chocolates to be attracted by you then you first need to believe that yes you can attract chocolates in life and then the second steps needs to be applied is that the essence of having the chocolate has to be created in our mind and we need to again and again recollect this same thought of having achieved the desired chocolates and we have to imagine yourself eating them. This leads to the manifestations of chocolate which is caused by the ORA that is created around you while you are recollecting the essence of chocolates again and again in your mind. But we need to understand that Law of attraction isn't just the manifestation of what we want in our life but it is a series of things that is required to be done together for several days, months or sometimes even years. The duration depends on the thing we are trying to manifest in our life. Manifestation is not something like we close our eyes and imagine of something we want and the desired thing magically appears in our life. There are certain techniques out there in the world that teaches you how to attract or manifest things but nobody have ever thought you what exactly happens and why a thing which we have thought about in our mind comes in front of us in our life, or why even after trying we are not able to attract that particular thing in our life.

After years of research and self practices, I have become aware of the true reality behind the process of LAW OF ATTRACTION.

"It is not what we crave outside but it is something connected deep inside"

- Mahesh Chandnani

When I used to practice Law of attraction I had made these two books first was called as GOAL book, while another one was called as ACHIEVERS book. I used to make a list of things which I want in my life and I used to draw them in my goal book, if not draw then I used to stick paper cuttings or posters of my dreams which I wanted to achieve in life. Once these dreams would be achieved I used to transfer my dream from goal book to achievers book respectively as it was the proof of achievement to me. It was great fun to achieve as many goals from the goals book and then transfer them to the achievers book.

"Open yourself to the great world of DREAMS and choose a life you always wanted"

- Mahesh Chandnani

Many of these dreams were achieved but there would always be few which used to always remain in the goal book, these were the few dreams which were never completed or achieved by me in life. This used to always bother me as I used to think why the process of Law of attraction not responding to for these few dreams. The answer to this question is already given to you in the first few pages of this book, I have mentioned in 'message to you' section that all that we are destined for achieving in life we will be able to achieve them without much difficulty but things which we choose from Greed, Hate, Envy or any other negative emotion attached with the desired. that thing can never be achieved properly even after putting 100% of your efforts you may deliberately attract that particular thing in life but it may have its own share of consequences that you will have to suffer.

This may either harm you or any other person close to you. It is like a supermarket sale which offers you to avail something free on the purchase of some minimum amount of merchandises. We end up buying unwanted stuff just to get the free material as we have liked it and want to achieve it. Similarly in life we have to pay a price if we are artificially creating something out of greed or other negative emotions attached, it may harm you or make you regret later for attracting it in your life. If you attract bad for someone or want to attract something just to show others how rich or famous you are in your life then you are attracting bad for yourselves which will manifest worst in life for you. What I am explaining now will look unrealistic to you but it does occur with its own space and time. If you have attracted bad for someone or you just have attracted something to show off in front of other people then for this behavior will pay a price later in life as by showing of your skills of attraction you are just willing to prove that others are less capable then you which is a negative emotion. It wouldn't be sooner but someday in your life you will come across a situation where you will be treated the same way as you used to treat others. That would be the time when you will realize your mistake you had done back then and would regret doing it then as it is causing you this problem. This kind of thing happens to everyone in life and it is called the **KARMIC CYCLE.** This Karmic cycle has a connection with law of attraction as in karmic cycle what we do in life gives us what we will deserve in future and in law of attraction it is who we are in the present gives us what we will deserve in future. I had been using Law of attraction in my life to get many things into my life being unaware of my emotions attached to it. This has let me suffer many times in life as I had to pay the price for what I had attracted. Learning how to attract things is very easy in life and can be practiced by everyone in this world but knowing how it is done and why one should use it, is something one needs to discover themselves in life. I have made that discovery all by myself and I will share with you the process that lies behind Law of attraction. But before you learn about the process that makes law of attraction work you need to first understand the importance of learning to classify the different emotions attached with the thing we attract in life. it is a small exercise where all you need to ask yourself is 'will my process of attraction for this particular thing cause harm to me or anybody else whom I know in this world' you need to ask this question to yourself before attracting anything in your life. The only reason we ask this question to us is that we do not want to harm any human being of this world and be tagged as selfish for life.

> **"Life gives us enough experiences to learn and understand our mistakes"**
>
> **- Mahesh Chandnani**

If the answer to the above question asked is a yes then your emotion is negative but if the answer to the question asked above is no then there is a positive emotion which is attached to your dreams.

NOTE: You can refer to the page '17' of this book for the reference of positive and negative emotion.

The memory of our mind is stored with respect to emotions attached to it. Similarly what we want to have in our future has an emotion attached to it. We attract things with particular emotion attached with it in our life. We have been attracting both positively as well as negatively in life as we have not been aware of this fact, now that we know it we can easily differentiate between our Desires.

Let me share with you how, you can learn to upgrade for happiness in your life. We have learned a lot of things from four different stages of learning but in our life now we are in the fifth stage of learning. We have become aware of our knowledge which we have gained from four stages of learning and now in the fifth stage of learning we need to learn something which is equally important for life. This fifth stage of learning helps us choose the right path, which always has been waiting for us. This path of truth enfolds in front of us making us realize how important our life really is. This path of truth shows us the true purpose of being born. It also shows us the direction we need to take being our true self in order to find happiness in our life.

A map is required for us to reach our destination but until the stage four of learning we do not know where our destination actually is? We have only learnt till now is to attract things positively but is this our main goal in life? Will you be just sitting inside your house attracting things to happen throughout your life? Or you would want to add some meaning to your life? There are very few people all over the world who get to understand this 5% of their personality which comes from the stage five of learning. Your personality depends on which stage you stop yourself form learning if you live a negative life it's the third stage you stopped learning about yourself and you missed out choosing your real personality. If you stop learning after knowing how you can attract things in life by using law of attraction then you stopped yourself from learning in the fourth stage. If you continue leaning about yourself even after the stage four of learning then you become a perfect identity because you have now learnt all about yourself with respect to the world which is outside you. People are just left with the knowledge they have from only four stages of learning. You can easily find these people around as they are the once whom we see talking about law of attraction in their lives and after few years of their living these same bunch of people have forgotten what law of attraction was in their life. This is a pretty common phenomenon all over the world, we see people whom we once saw happy and enjoying their lives using this technique have become bored, unhappy and goalless in life. These are the people who have given up on all their dreams and are just living on things they had once created for themselves as they feel lost after creating what was desired by them in life. Loosing yourself after achieving your goals in life is a possibility because you have spent all your powers on the desired thing and now that it has come true you are happy as your efforts have paid off. This happiness about achieving this dream is not going to be with you all your life, the fact is that it is not even going to be there for a longer period of time.

Everything 'THAT IS' will always become 'THAT WAS' in life"

- Mahesh Chandnani

There would be a time in life where you would not have anything to feel happy about as the thing you are happy now will make you feel ordinary later. The excitement will diminish soon and life will ask you a question **ARE YOU WORTH YOUR LIVING?** The reasons you will not have any answer to this question will be the same feeling that you had felt on entering the stage four of learning. This is a materialistic world which has a lot of materials surrounding our human life. Every individual is dependent on these verities of materialistic cravings that are manmade in nature.

If you desire to own a car it is going to be manmade in nature, if you want to owe a lavish house for yourself it is again going to be man made in nature, if you want to buy the latest smart phone to use daily, it is again manmade in nature. Similarly, if I ask you to list down things you want in your life right now, all the lists will contain man made things which we human's believe makes us happy. Even though you are able to achieve these things, happiness will only be temporary for you.

These are the things desired by the today's generation throughout the world in their life	
Latest phones	Own house
Big brand cars	Laptops
Sports bikes	Digital cameras
Latest fashion	High paid jobs
Easy money	Exotic vacations
Casual relationships	Parties
Personal Freedom	Grand Lifestyle

"ALL THAT WE DESIRE FROM OUTER WORLD GIVES US TEMPORARY HAPPPINESS AS IT IS MANMADE IN NATURE"

- Mahesh Chandnani

Irrespective of whom we are in life? Or what we have in our destiny? Or where our destination is? We young generation of this modern world has started being governed by the EVIL power commonly known as EGO. Ego is defined by me as the **EVIL GOVERNING OVER**. EGO is determined by people when they show off what they have in their life. The more things you have the bigger is your EGO. In today's modern world EGO is used as self defense. People without EGO are ill treated or constantly used by others for selfish reasons. People have become vulnerable in their life, even a good soul has to show some EVIL traits to be protected from other evil beings in this world. Evil nature in human beings is the selfish side of us. It is this selfishness inside us that makes us do a lot of EVIL things to others including our loved once. Ego forces us to attract things that others have this leads to harm the person to whom that particular thing belonged to. Ego is a negative emotion that we choose to keep within us to use as self defense. EGO doesn't stop here it has more things attached to it. When we begin our stage three of learning we realize there is something special in every individual, for which that particular person starts being known for in the school and high school. I am talking about talents in sports, dance, singing, playing musical instruments, scoring well in academics, etc. you may have known at least one person from your life that would have been known for one of the talents mentioned above. We as humans always crib in life for something we do not have without appreciating what we do have in life. Ego is always present within us it is a part of our personality since we are born and it is discovered by us during the second and the third stage of learning. We come to know about EGO during the time when we discover our hidden talent in life. When we are praised by people all around us for that particular talent we are gifted for, we get used to listening praises from people and we soon start craving for being more praised by people all over. This emerging demand for getting praised by people is created by our EGO within. Our EGO is nothing more but a false reality which is created just to feel good about our self. It makes you feel that you are the ultimate being and nobody else can be like you are. When our positive emotions attached to a memory become negative it is EGO that is responsible for it. Let me give you an example from childhood memories, children are not aware of ego but you can see and understand how innocently they portrait it in front of everyone. If you see two children doing funny stuff in front of their parents just to gain their attention, if one of the two gets the attention from their parents for their funny behavior the other child doesn't feel good about it, he or she just tries to copy what first child had done or simply gets angry and starts crying. EGO isn't a big deal in our childhood but the story is completely different in second or third stage of learning, if we get jealous of somebody being better than us the next thing that flows in our mind is to become like that person or just take his place in life. We often do this in life where we always compare our life with other person's life. This is what we have already discussed in the third and fourth stage of learning. In the fifth stage of learning we also get a chance to discover the truth behind EGO. Instead of appreciating other person's talents, we change the positive thought into a negative thought. The only thing that happens by doing this is that we harm ourselves from inside that cause us to surround ourselves with the unwanted negativity. This negativity stops us from exploring our own creativeness. **One needs to get rid of this fake identity created by him (EGO) so that one can pursue the destined creativity and become as original as one was born.** Nobody in this world are same human beings, one person cannot match the originality of the other person. The original person who has discovered his true path leads himself towards destination of life.

These are the few examples of people who reached their destination of life discovering their true paths.

1) Jesus Christ
2) Gautama Buddha
3) Michael Jackson
4) Mahatma Gandhi
5) Warne Buffets
6) Sachin Tendulkar
7) Amitab Bachchan
8) Nelson Mandela
9) Mahesh Chandnani
The list is endless

"SUCCESS HAPPENS TO US WHEN WE STOP FIGHTING WITH OUR OWN DESTINY"

- Mahesh Chandnani

You may want to believe that whatever happens to your life happens because of your efforts, even the world's best phrases of all time states that 'GOD HELPS THOSE WHO HELPS THEMSELVES' but haven't you seen people becoming successful when they aren't even trying. Achieving success is an endless journey as one cannot define it universally. 'SUCCEESS IS AN EVENT THAT IS VERY PEROSNAL' every individual describes success in different ways, it again depends on what your destiny has for you. The reason people fail to understand what success is in their life is because they aren't able to achieve it. They are always finding it in a wrong place. Success isn't what you achieve in this materialistic world, the cars the house the money are all the secondary aspects of the world. Success is something that can only be felt from within. It is our EGO that makes you believe that you are known by the things you have in your life. If these things are taken away from you then you will be unable to recognize yourself. You cannot achieve success by having different identities, one being the identity you are born with and other being the fake identity that is created within called EGO.

To achieve success in life we need to forget our fake side of personality and become aware of our true potentials in life.

"Things you fail to do in life, is a signal for you to realize that GOD has something better in his mind for you"

- Mahesh Chandnani

We humans with our mind can control many things in our life but half of the time our mind is filled with a lot of confusions with respect to many things in our life. These confusions are created by us because we lack confidence in choosing what is best for us in our own life. More than half of our life is spend in confusions and later we always find our self complaining that we wasted our life by not choosing the right path present in front of us that could have taken us to success. We all have our destination in life. We all are born to reach there in our life's journey but we are not able to.

"Best feeling in life is when you realize where you stand in life and how FAR is your Destination"

- Mahesh Chandnani

We are not able to reach there because in this life our mind is filled with confusions due to which we are lost in life. In order to reach our destination we need to be confident with our personality. This will help us choose our path properly but we cannot achieve success in life without learning what I m going to teach you in this next chapter.

MEDITATE SELF SUCCESS

MEDITATE FOR

Meditate
Self
Success

You may have heard the term visualization. It is most commonly used in the process of law of attraction. What it really does is helps us build the atmosphere around us so that we can easily believe in the things we want to achieve in life. In the previous chapter I showed you two important steps which were used In the process of law of attraction.

These two steps are:

1) **Believe in your dream.**
2) **magine already you have achieved it.**

These two steps when performed together are equally known as Visualization. We visualize what we want in our life when we close our eyes and imagine achieving what we want in our mind. This process changes the ORA around us making us feel more powerful and positive about our belief. Law of attraction asks us to visualize on our dreams more than three times in a day. This makes us feel really good about our own self as the reality in which we currently live in becomes history and we start connecting ourselves with the future life.

This is how ORA surround us while visualizing

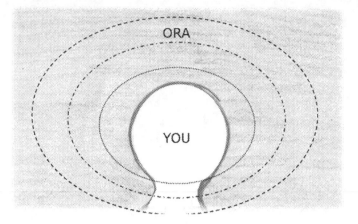

Whenever we travel around the city we find people having different ORA's around them. This is because they differ in thoughts with us, many a times we do not have to look outside as we find such people inside our house only. You find your own family members having different ORA's around them. So it really doesn't matter what other people think about you as we have learnt in fourth stage of learning that we shouldn't be concerned about other people's perspective. We should clearly indicate our thoughts to be powerful enough to be able to achieve what is desired by you in life.

When we sit at one quite place closing our eyes and thinking about our dreams, we feel the positivity around us which is created by the ORA. This 'ORA' is nothing else but the Energy that surrounds us making us feel lighter and happier. We feel blessed by the power present in the energy that is all around our face while visualizing.

What is this Energy?, where does it come from?, why it makes us feel positive and keep us happy?, also when this ORA is created once it can always be created again and again without much efforts. Why does this happen?, How it leads to manifestation? These were questions that made me research, just to find the answers and share it with the world.

This world we live in is a part of the universe, the entire universe functions on the Energy, which is beyond understanding level of human mankind. Why does earth revolves around the sun? How is the sun the ultimate source of light? How does one calculate time using rotations of the Earth? Etc. all these questions make us very inferior in front of the universe as we are just a tiny creation created by the creator, who has also created this universe. And we humans believe that we can create a new world or can change the world we live in while we cannot even control our own life. This entire universe is running on this energy which gets created around us when we visualize. In science terminology we may consider this energy as a frequency that can be measured inside or outside of our body. This energy is called COSMIC ENERGY. Cosmic energy is universally present all over. Great scientists have tried to solve the mystery behind the source of this energy but they have concluded the energy by revealing this law of energy to us.

"ENERGY CAN NEITHER BE CREATED NOR BE DESTROYED IT SIMPLY CHANGE FROM ONE FORM TO ANOTHER"

- ISSAC NEWTON

This is what happens in the case of manifestation. To explain this process we will have to learn something that is more powerful than visualization, the process, we will learn is called **MEDITATION.**

But before we learn something about meditation, we will first need to understand what connection we share as humans with the universal energy. All the things we see in this world were created by this energy, including us. We all feel this energy within us when we wake up in the morning, the process by which we grasp all the energy for living is called **sleeping**. While we are sleeping consciously our subconscious mind and all other body organs are working to their fullest, while we are lost in the world of thoughts called dreams are body recharges itself with this UNIVERSAL ENERGY. It is a fact that we are also a part of this universal energy. Every living being has this energy which he has not created by himself and he can't destroy it as well. It is this energy which lies within every living being present in this world. This unknown source of energy is called **SOUL. Soul** is present in every living organism, if this soul goes missing from the body the body no longer called living.

SOUL = UNIVERSAL ENERGY PRESENT WITHIN.

It can neither be created nor be destroyed. It can only be transformed from one form to another. After a human dies his soul is again transformed into new body, it is the process of life and death that continues since the time humans have existed.

The truth is that the soul which is present in the form of energy inside our body after death it goes back to its source which is the universal energy. All we humans have been doing is multiplying this universal energy present in us by giving birth to our children. The souls in children are just the universal Energies which have been passed to them from their parents. Every living species has a SOUL (universal energy) that is further transferred to the child from both their parents. Child gets maximum amount of SOUL (universal energy) from **MOTHER**.

Energy is universal therefore the soul is also universal. This world was created by the transformation of this universal energy which has evolved taking different kind of forms, such as living beings and other non living materials in the world. Non living materials were created to support living beings as we humans require non living materials to survive for our living, the three basic necessity for living (food, clothing and shelter) are all non living in nature. When we talk about living and non living things present in this world we realize that it all has been created by something that is beyond our understanding level as even we are his creations. We do not know who the creator is but we all call him **GOD**. **God** as described by humans is all powerful, all knowledgeable. He is present everywhere, etc. You may find millions of definitions given by people all over the world when you ask them to describe GOD? But the truth is that **'GOD is the ultimate creator of everything'** and this will always remain the same. I share this knowledge about GOD is to make you understand how you can actually feel the presence of the creator with the help of **MEDITATION**. **Meditation** isn't just a technique of relaxation. It is a complete new world within us which is left unseen by billions of people as they spend their lives ignoring this world that lies within. If GOD is present everywhere then he is outside us, he is inside us, he is in you, he is within me but what is there within us is the universal energy(SOUL) therefore GOD IS the universal energy which is found in me and found in You. One may say that how can GOD be Energy, while others can say that GOD cannot be categorized as the ENERGY. But let me explain you why GOD is this universal ENERGY.

1) **Energy is universal, so is GOD**
2) **Energy is found everywhere, so is GOD.**
3) **Energy cannot be seen, even GOD isn't seen.**
4) **There is no source for energy, source of GOD can't be defined either.**
5) **Energy can be felt. Even presence of GOD can be felt.**
6) **Energy can't be created by humans even GOD can't be created by humans.**
7) **ENERGY cannot be destroyed, even GOD cannot be destroyed.**

GOD hasn't created Energy but he himself is the Energy that runs this universe. One can feel GOD with the help of MEDITATION. The ORA which surrounds us while we visualize is multiplied many times surrounding entire body.

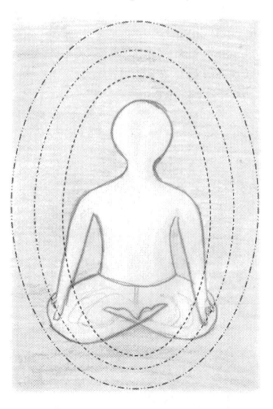

This happens when we sit for meditation.

When we sit for meditation and continue focusing on our breath for a longer period of time until we notice breath reducing. When Energy (GOD) surrounds us while meditating we feel our breath frequency reducing. This is the sign of relaxation which is caused by the presence of Energy (GOD) around you. At this time you are ready to let the energy (GOD) around you to become a part of you. Allowing Energy (GOD) to penetrate inside you, we focus on the upper most part of our body that is our skull. Energy (GOD) enters our body from the tip of our skull and starts flowing all over. Our face is the first place where the Energy (GOD) gets filled making it glow with positivity, slowly the Energy (GOD) flows deeper to our chest, abdomen, shoulders, hands, back and leg. Soon every portion of our body gets covered with Energy (GOD) leading it to create **ONENESS.** ONENESS is created when the two separate worlds of the inside and outside becomes the same. This makes us feel completely away from all our worries as what we feel at present is a different story. At this stage your inside and your outside has become same, there is no more difference between your inner world and the outer world. It is now when you can feel the presence of Energy (GOD) inside you as well as outside you. This stage is called ONENESS as you become one with GOD. Once you have achieved this in your life, you realize that all the struggles in life are useless. There is absolutely nothing that creates stress for us in life, stress is just a word given by us to describe a person's life having multiple tensions. This is how energy enters our body and we experience ONENESS with GOD.

ONENESS WITH GOD

GOD has not invented stress it is manmade in nature, we have lived for thousands of years without stress but in modern world we all share a stressful life. People are running behind money and other materials that make them live a fake life without being happy. Everything in today's world is just Business nobody tries to discover what their true nature should be. Life is getting shorter day by day. The only reason behind people dying so early in life is due to Stress. Human beings take a lot of tensions about many different things at a time which results in causing them stress in life. These tensions are not even important in life. When we discover this ONENESS with GOD we learn to stop giving importance to stress. All our suffering in our life's journey seems to be coming to an end. This is the sixth stage of learning in our life which makes us learn about things that we have never imagined. We learn to solve our problems all by ourselves, our thoughts purifying automatically, our life starts improving and problems are no longer permanent in life. We have now learnt to jump over obstacles. Slowly we come over every bit of troubles and finally reach our goals planned by our destiny.

The struggle for success has now become history.

The ONENESS with GOD makes us the perfect of what we are. All we are now supposed to do is **TRUST** in what GOD has in life for us. Trust was the first thing we had ever learnt in life and now we need to trust our DESTINY by TRUSTING in GOD. One may ask how can we trust our destiny as it is nowhere to be found, to trust our destiny we need to trust god, by trusting in god I mean trusting in the energy that surrounds us while meditation. We need to do as GOD shows us or tells us to do when we are in ONENESS during MEDITATION. We need to practice ONENESS with GOD by the process of MEDITATION every day as it gives us the answers to all our questions. If we are not able to do it daily then at least 3 times a week can help us to get solutions to all our problems. It shows us the right path. It always makes us aware of our true potentials. We now start living the life we were born for, without any tensions, worries or obstacles we learn to be happy in every situation of life.

"Uniting with the CREATOR we get the power to CREATE our DREAMS come TRUE"

- **Mahesh Chandnani**

With the help of the creator we become the creator of our dreams and we learn to create our own world for us. We get the power to manifest everything that is needed for us in our life. We achieve whatever we require at this moment in life, things start happening faster and better for us. Life becomes very easy for us to live with happiness.

Two things you should always remember
1) ONENESS is achieved only when you are willing to achieve it in your life.
2) TRUST you inner saying as it will lead you to a life you have always imagined.

If you start practicing ONENESS you would soon reach a stage where you would no longer have to make the list of things you want in your life. Everything will happen to you automatically.

Once we are at the stage of ONENESS with GOD, we have many thoughts and desires that we share with him. GOD then takes these thoughts in the form of bubbles from us to find a perfect match. When we are in the process of ONENESS our thoughts and problems are taken away from us. These thoughts and problems are taken in the form of a bubble that GOD takes with him, to find the solution of the problem or to manifest our wishes. It all happens during the process of meditation. We all send these bubbles with GOD asking him to solve our problems or granting us our wishes. GOD takes these thoughts and releases them in the universe to find the perfect match for us, when the match is found the magic of manifestation occurs. Let me explain you this with the help of example. When we desire Love in our life, we put this thought as a bubble and send it with GOD. We may be wanting it from a specific someone we have in mind But GOD always grants our wishes in **PAIRS**. For GOD what is desired by us is LOVE and if this same LOVE is desired by someone around us then the wish would be granted. It may be someone we know or someone we might be introduced to in future. . **All the manifestation occurs in pairs.**

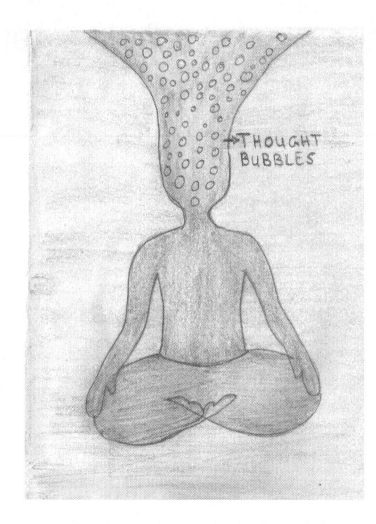

Your thoughts are taken away in the form of bubbles

To understand this consider there are three people

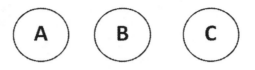

If A desires LOVE in his life but wants it from B in specific but B doesn't want love in her life then the manifestation will not occur as the pair wouldn't be formed. But if A yet desires love in his life but is clinging to get it from B then he would result in making himself unhappy and not satisfied and blame GOD for not helping him to find love.

That is why GOD always works in pair as GOD believes in granting two common wishes at a time.

Two different individual wishes = one manifestation

In the same example if A desired love and there was C who also desired love at the same time then the manifestation occurs in our life as GOD grants both the wishes together with one manifestation. A will be granted to C and C will be granted to A making them a manifested couple. We should always keep our selves open, when our wish is granted in life, god always makes sure whatever we want is arranged for us as soon as possible. If we have a wish that is not fulfilled yet, it is because GOD has not found a match for it yet. This does not mean that our wish would never be fulfilled, it only means that we will have to wait until its match is found. Once the match would be found for our wish, manifestation will occur automatically in our life. it happens to all of us we all have some wishes in life that are manifested after a long time and we end up saying that this wish was desired by me for a longer period of time and it has finally happened.

SOME THOUGHTS TAKE TIME, SOME ARE EASILY MANIFESTED IN LIFE, DREAMS DO COME TRUE BUT THERE IS A PROCESS ONE NEEDS TO FOLLOW IN LIFE, MEDITATION MAKES US ONE WITH GOD AND GOD LEADS US TO A LIFE WE HAVE ALWAYS IMAGINED. Let us all recollect everything learnt from this book and apply with, what I going to teach you in this next chapter that will help you to achieve everything you want in our life.

"DREAMS COME TRUE, YOU CREATE THEM,
WHEN YOU LEARN TO EXPLORE THE
PHILOSOPHY OF ACHIEVERS WITHIN YOU"

- Mahesh Chandnani

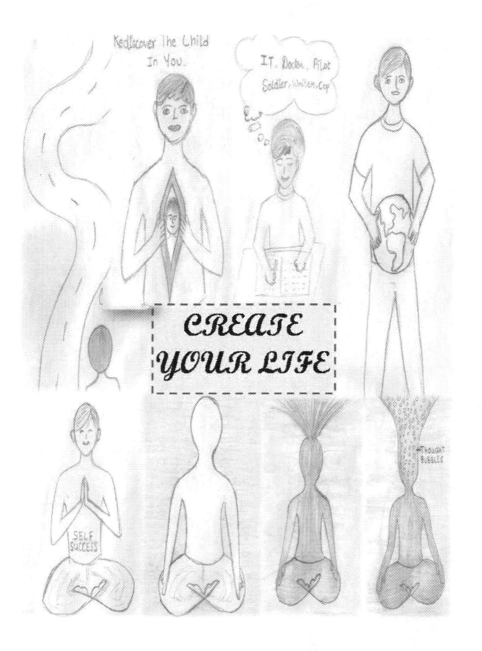

CREATE YOUR
LIFE

**LEARN THIS PROCESS
AND THEN JUST
SIT AND MEDITATE**

- Mahesh Chandnani

Create Your Life

This last chapter of this book will help you summarize everything you have learnt from reading this book. It would also teach you something that we learn in life after achieving the VI stage of learning it is the knowledge that we gain from our world within. It will help you quickly recollect all the important teachings you need to remember in your life in order to be Successful.

We all are the beings of one ultimate creator. We owe him everything we have in our life but in return he only wants one thing from us **'TRUST'**. We have spent entire life without trusting our own DESTINY, this ignoring attitude of our life have made us realized that we are not so happy. Our life has always brought us to a stage where we feel lost in our life, the hope we live for is taken away from us and all is left to us is suffering and misery. This is the time when we look up to sky asking the GOD. Why you gave me this life which is full of suffering, it would have been better if I would have not born to live a life that has nothing good for me.

We feel bad about ourselves when we see people around us being happy. All we do is crib about our life and create more sadness and misery for our own self. Without realizing what we are doing we keep on doing this for years until we finally die.

If our life was made to suffer then we wouldn't have ever experienced happiness in our life. Our world is filled with happiness being all around us. So why, we then complain to god for sadness in life. Happiness and sadness are like two different sides of a COIN. If you feel you are sad in life then all you need to do is flip the coin to the happy part of life. Every day we have many different experiences based of thousands of situations. These situations are then attached with the human emotion that makes it a memory. These memories are all stored in our subconscious mind.

Our subconscious mind stores all the memories we have generated since birth, it is not different form our conscious mind, both are equal parts of our brain. Every human being is born with a brain therefore every human being has a conscious and a subconscious mind. Our subconscious mind is responsible for all the tasks which are conducted in our body while our conscious mind is sleeping. Our world of dreams which we see while sleeping is caused by subconscious mind in order to keep us in a resting position, so that all our internal processes gets a peaceful time to finish their work before we wake up in the morning. Another aspect of our life is that we all have the universal energy within us which is the secret of our living. It is this universal energy that helps our body to execute all our internal processes like digestion system, Nervous system, respiratory system, cardio vascular system, etc. you may say that all these systems have their respective organs work independently. Science has proven how all the systems work in our body, putting them into separate categories but what science fails to understand is the source that keeps everything running in our BODY.

Let me show you how our body works

Science may say that every system of our body is individually responsible in executing their process. But the truth is we require resources from nature to survive, one of the basic necessities in life is FOOD and Food for us comes from nature. If you are a vegetarian or a non vegetarian you will ultimately depend on the natural resources. When we eat food our digestive system starts its process, but it cannot function unless our Brain signals it to start working, our brain is connected to every single part of our body by our NERVOUS SYSTEM but our nervous system cannot function unless It is receiving blood which is pumped by our Heart and supplied to each part of our body by our CARDIO VASCULAR SYSTEM, our Heart is continuously working in our body but again it cannot function unless the blood is purified in our RESPIRATORY SYSTEM. Our respiratory system brings the carbon dioxide out from our body by exhaling it out from our nostrils inhaling back oxygen. Oxygen is present in the atmosphere which is again part of the Nature. The food we eat is grown on trees which have their own system that inhales carbon dioxide which is released by us and exhales oxygen which is required by living beings for their survival. other food sources which we humans rely on are animals, animals also have similar systems like human beings, even they survive on oxygen like humans. Our body functions are all designed dependent on one and other and they are all together responsible to keep us alive, but what science fails to identify is the source that keeps everything in all the living beings (humans, plants and animals) working perfectly fine in our body. That source which is responsible is none other than the **UNIVERSAL EVERGY** which is present in our body and we call it our **SOUL.** This universal energy is also present in nature in the form of OXYGEN for human beings and animals while it is present in the form of carbon dioxide for plants.

When we sit for meditation our oxygen intake reduces this happens because there is the presence of cosmic energy around. This cosmic energy is the universal energy that is present in the nature and is full of OXYGEN. So there is ample amount of OXYGEN which is made available around us during the time of meditation. Therefore the intake of oxygen is the purest during meditation this is why our breathing reduces while meditating. It allows our respiratory organs to relax allowing all other systems and their respective organs to relax with it because everything in our body is connected with our respiratory system. This reduces the demand for oxygen in our body as every system of body is relaxing because we have surrendered ourselves to the cosmic energy which is the purest form of OXYGEN around us. This allows the energy within (**SOUL**) to meet the energy around us (**OXYGEN**). The question here is, if the energy in our body and the energy present outside the body are same then how and when does this outside energy comes into our body and what happens to energy after we die. When we are in our mother's womb we are growing and living on her ENERGY. All the required resources like blood and oxygen are provided to us with the help of newly formed placenta and umbilical cord. Entire 9 months of pregnancy the baby grows on mother's energy (OXYGEN). Baby's respiratory system develops inside the womb but it starts functioning after head is out during delivery. When we talk about OXYGEN being the Energy around us we also come to know that, it is this OXYGEN that is required by us for our SURVIVAL. The soul that we have within us enters in our body with the first breath we take during the time of our mom's labor and the soul exits our body when we take the last breath of our life. This makes us come to a conclusion that what lies within is nothing else but the UNIVERSAL ENERGY that is found around us. **OXYGEN** (energy around us) = **SOUL** (energy within).

Our universe runs on ENERGY —> GOD is himself the universal energy —> when we sit to meditate there is energy that gets accumulated around us —> this energy is called cosmic energy as it is full OXYGEN —> OXYGEN is the form of universal energy for human beings —> ENERGY within human beings is called SOUL —> the human soul require oxygen to survive —> Soul enters with first breath and leaves with the last —> therefore **SOUL = OXYGEN.**

There is no need to be confused about the whole thing. It is really simple to understand how well our creator has made this world for us. First he made the entire universe and then to run this universe he transformed himself into ENERGY. This energy can neither be destroyed nor be created but can only be transformed from one form to another. GOD is this energy that is present everywhere around us. The reason we can feel GOD when we meditate is because it is the only time we spend alone with us. When GOD enters our body he makes sure everything within us is perfect. If you observer yourself while meditating you will become aware of the painful areas in your body, this pain is created by GOD to cure negativity away from within. What is present around and within us during the time of meditation is OXYGEN. Oxygen in nature is the form of universal energy that is very essential for human beings and is required the most to survive. We keep finding GOD everywhere but he is within. God is the energy present in this world but Energy is available in the form of OXYGEN for us therefore GOD himself is the ENERGY that we BREATHE IN. You breathe in GOD but you yet struggle to find him.

"WORSHIP YOURSELF AS YOU ARE SENT IN THIS WORLD TO LIVE A LIFE YOU ALWAYS WANTED"

- Mahesh Chandnani

What we learn in our life is the knowledge that stays with us for our entire life span. What we are and where our destination is are the two concepts that have been cleared to you with the help of this learning graph. It shows us everything we learn in all different stages of learning. This learning graph together builds our personality that we portrait in front of people but if you total the percentages given below it is 40%+5%+25%+15%+5%=90%

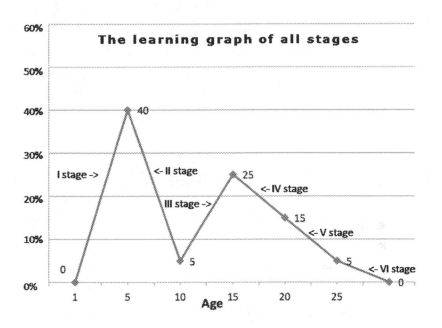

90% of our personality is learnt by us from the outer world of existence but the remaining 10% of our personality comes for us from within. The sixth stage of learning shown in the graph above is the beginning of our journey within. All that is around us is been explored by us till we reach fifth stage of learning, there is nothing else left to be explore in the outer world for us therefore we have to look within for the answers that we learn in our life is from the sixth and the seventh stage of learning.

"ANSWERS TO ALL GOOD AND EVIL LIES WITHIN"

- Mahesh Chandnani

The graph shown below explains us how we learn things from the two different worlds in our life.

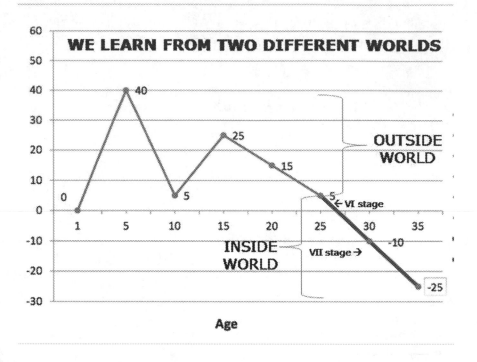

YOU ARE INCHAREGED OF HAVING A POSITIVE MIND

- **Mahesh Chandnani**

TO CREATE YOUR FUTURE CONSIDER YOURSELF AS A HERO IN YOUR LIFE. ALL YOU NEED TO DO NOW IS WRITE YOUR OWN STORY. Choosing from who you are and you want to be.

ANGEL and DEVIL side within you

You have the choice to choose whom you want to be

DESTINY has everything for you with the knowledge learnt from this book you need to now **CREATE YOUR LIFE.**

Upcoming Books in Future

DO WE NEED GOD – this book is a life story of a young BOY named CHARLIE, who experiences 7 different religions in his life and grows asking this question **DO WE NEED GOD IN LIFE?** The story revolves around him, to find an answer that makes him ultimately discover the path of spirituality.

HEART ECLIPSE – this is a story of teenage love. Falling in love during our teenage is most common in our life. Our heart is full of love at this age but we are not always successful, this story tells us how a heart can break leading to a heart eclipse.

PHILOSOPHY OF ACHIEVERS – This book is going to be a easy guide for achieving success in life. it will show people how to be successful in life by using three simple steps known as DUM principle.

REDISCOVER THE CHILD IN YOU - this book is a story of guy who is frustrated of his current working life and desperately wants to change it, the story is about how he realizes happiness and what makes him REDISCOVER THE CHILD WITHIN.

BE DAY DREAMER – this book is a comparison between the world of dreams and our dreams. What we dream at night is called world of dreams but if we dream to achieve its called DAY dreamer. The book shows us the detailed examples of how a dream occurs in night and why we have dreams while sleeping, it also explains why having a dream during the day is more beneficial then night dreams.

UPGRADE FOR HAPPINESS – this is a story of a young guy who has lost all happiness in his life. It is the story of his journey describing his struggles to find the true meaning of life, as he believes to find happiness one should have a meaningful life.

ONENESS, BECOME ONE WITH GOD – we live in the universe that is created by the one creator. But our entire life we believe that our creator is superior to us and we cannot be one with him. What we fail to understand is GOD has sent us in this world to have all we want in our life, then why we suffer with pain and misery, this book explores the actual essence of GOD giving us indebt knowledge about how we can be one with him. Book also shows us the path leading towards GOD. Showing us how a man can become one with him.

Future References

Facebook

https://www.facebook.com/MaheshChandnaniPage

Twitter

https://twitter.com/M_CHANDNANI

Instagram

https://instagram.com/mahesh_chandnani

Wordpress

https://maheshchandnani.wordpress.com

YouTube

https://www.youtube.com/c/maheshchandnanipage

Websites

1. www.creatorofyourdreams.com

2. www.maheshchandnani.com

Printed in the United States
By Bookmasters